For Love of Country

For Love

BEACON PRESS
BOSTON

Debating the Limits
of Patriotism

# of Country

Martha C. Nussbaum
with Respondents

Edited by Joshua Cohen

Beacon Press
25 Beacon Street
Boston, Massachusetts 02108-2892
www.beacon.org

Beacon Press books
are published under the auspices of
the Unitarian Universalist Association of Congregations.

First digital-print edition 2002

Text design by Daniel Ochsner
Composition by Wilsted & Taylor

Library of Congress Cataloging-in-Publication Data
Nussbaum, Martha Craven, 1947–
For love of country : debating the limits of patriotism /
Martha C. Nussbaum with respondents ; edited by Joshua Cohen.
p.   cm.
ISBN 0-8070-4313-3 (pbk.)
1. Internationalism. 2. Patriotism. I. Cohen, Joshua, 1951-. II. Title.
JC362.N87   1996
327.1´7—dc20   96-368

Contents

Joshua Cohen

Preface

In his great Riverside Church speech of April 1967, Martin Luther King Jr. declared his reasons for opposing the Vietnam War. The war was, he said, a disaster for Black Americans, poisonous for the country, and above all a nightmare "for victims of our nation and for those it calls enemy." Responding to moral demands that lie "beyond the calling of race or nation or creed," King said that he had come to speak for these "enemies." Speaking out was the "privilege and the burden of all of us who deem ourselves bound by allegiances and loyalties which are broader and deeper than nationalism and which go beyond our nation's self-defined goals and positions."

In her essay "Patriotism and Cosmopolitanism"—which provoked the debate recorded in this book—Martha Nussbaum defends the moral position to which King gave such powerful expression. According to this cosmopolitan outlook, our highest allegiance must be to the community of humankind, and the first principles of our practical thought must respect the equal worth of all members of that community. Cosmopolitanism is a controversial view, one tendency of moral thought opposed by outlooks that resist its ideal of world citizenship in the name of sensibilities and attachments rooted in group affiliation or national tradition. The responses to Nussbaum reflect these conflicting pulls, highlighting at once the complexity of these issues and the importance of their resolution.

This book, then, presents competing philosophies—first principles connected to conduct through complex links of historical circumstance, social location, and individual judgment. But as King's condemnation of the war demonstrates, those connections are no less real for being indirect. The disagreement about cosmopolitanism is practical as well as theoretical, with important implications for contemporary debate about protectionism, immigration, human rights, foreign intervention, development assistance, and what we should teach in our schools. In exploring the merits of cosmopolitanism as moral theory and personal conviction, Martha Nussbaum and her respondents join philosophical debate to public discussion, enriching each.

NUSSBAUM'S LEAD ESSAY FIRST APPEARED IN *BOSTON Review* (October/November 1994), along with twenty-nine replies. Eleven of those replies are included here, some substantially expanded, along with five new contributions. Decisions about which of the original replies to include required complex editorial judgments—largely about how to ensure the intellectual diversity required for successful debate. I am grateful to Martha Nussbaum, Andrew Hrycyna, and Deb Chasman for their advice in helping to make those judgments. And on behalf of all the contributors, I wish to express gratitude to Kim Van Dyke for her editorial assistance.

I

Patriotism

When anyone asked him where he came from, he said,
"I am a citizen of the world."

Diogenes Laertius, *Life of Diogenes the Cynic*

and Cosmopolitanism

I

In Rabindranath Tagore's novel *The Home and the World*, the young wife Bimala, entranced by the patriotic rhetoric of her husband's friend Sandip, becomes an eager devotee of the *Swadeshi* movement, which has organized a boycott of foreign goods. The slogan of the movement is *Bande Mataram* (Hail Motherland). Bimala complains that her husband, the cosmopolitan Hindu landlord Nikhil, is cool in his devotion to the cause:

> And yet it was not that my husband refused to support *Swadeshi*, or was in any way against the Cause. Only he had not been able wholeheartedly to accept the spirit of *Bande Mataram*.
>
> "I am willing," he said, "to serve my country; but my worship I reserve for Right which is far greater than my country. To worship my country as a god is to bring a curse upon it."

Americans have frequently supported the principle of *Bande Mataram*, giving the fact of being American a special salience in moral and political deliberation, and pride in a specifically American identity and a specifically American citizenship a special power among the motivations to political action. I believe, as do Tagore and his character Nikhil, that this emphasis on patriotic pride is both morally dangerous and, ultimately, subversive of some of the worthy goals patriotism sets out to serve—for example, the goal of national unity in devotion to worthy moral ideals of justice and equality. These goals, I shall argue, would be better served by an ideal that is in any case more adequate to our situation in the contemporary world, namely the very old ideal of the cosmopolitan, the person whose allegiance is to the worldwide community of human beings.

My articulation of these issues is motivated, in part, by my experience working on international quality-of-life issues in an institute for development economics connected with the United Nations. It is also motivated by the renewal of appeals to the nation, and national pride, in some recent discussions of American character and American education. In a well-known op-ed piece in the *New York Times* (13 February 1994), philosopher Richard Rorty urges Americans, especially the American left, not to disdain patriotism as a value, and indeed to give central importance to "the emotion of national pride" and "a sense of shared national identity." Rorty argues that we cannot even criticize ourselves well unless we also "rejoice" in our American identity and define ourselves fundamentally in terms of that identity. Rorty seems to hold that the primary alternative to a politics based on patriotism and national identity is what he calls a "politics of difference," one based on internal divisions among America's ethnic, racial, religious, and other subgroups. He nowhere considers the possibility of a more international basis for political emotion and concern.

This is no isolated case. Rorty's piece responds to and defends Sheldon Hackney's recent call for a "national conversation" to discuss American identity.[1] As a participant in its early phase, I was made vividly aware that the project, as initially conceived,[2] proposed an inward-looking task, bounded by the borders of the nation, rather than considering ties of obligation and commitment that join America to the rest of the world. As with Rorty's piece, the primary contrast drawn in the project was between a politics based on ethnic and racial and religious difference and a politics based on a shared national identity. What we share as both rational and mutually dependent human beings was simply not on the agenda.

One might wonder, however, how far the politics of nationalism really is from the politics of difference. *The Home and the World* (better known, perhaps, in Satyajit Ray's haunting film of the same title) is a tragic story of the defeat of a reasonable and principled cosmopolitanism by the forces of nationalism and ethnocentrism. I believe that Tagore sees deeply when he observes that, at bottom, nationalism and ethnocentric particularism are not alien to one another, but akin—that to give support to nationalist sentiments subverts, ultimately, even the values that hold a nation together, because it substitutes a colorful idol for the substantive universal values of justice and right. Once someone has said, I am an Indian first, a citizen of the world second, once he or she has made that morally questionable move of self-definition by a morally irrelevant characteristic, then what, indeed, will stop that person from saying, as Tagore's characters so quickly learn to say, I am a Hindu first, and an Indian second, or I am an upper-caste landlord first, and a Hindu second? Only the cosmopolitan stance of the landlord Nikhil—so boringly flat in the eyes of his young wife Bimala and his passionate nationalist friend Sandip—has the promise of transcending these divisions, because only this stance asks us to give our first allegiance to what is morally good—and that which, being good, I can commend as such to all human beings.

Proponents of nationalism in politics and in education frequently make a weak concession to cosmopolitanism. They may argue, for example, that although nations should in general base education and political deliberation on shared national values, a commitment to basic human rights should be part of any national education system, and that this commitment will in a sense hold many nations together.[3] This seems to be a fair comment on practical reality; and the emphasis on human rights is certainly necessary for a world in which nations interact all the time on terms (let us hope) of justice and mutual respect.

But is it sufficient? As students here grow up, is it sufficient for them to learn that they are above all citizens of the United States but that they ought to respect the basic human rights of citizens of India, Bolivia, Nigeria, and Norway? Or should they—as I think—in addition to giving special attention to the history and current situation of their own nation, learn a good deal more than they frequently do about the rest of the world in which they live, about India and Bolivia and Nigeria and Norway and their histories, problems, and comparative successes? Should they learn only that citizens of India have equal basic human rights, or should they also learn about the problems of hunger and pollution in India, and the implications of these problems for the larger issues of global hunger and global ecology? Most important, should they be taught that they are, above all, citizens of the United States, or should they instead be taught that they are, above all, citizens of a world of human beings, and that, while they happen to be situated in the United States, they have to share this world with the citizens of other countries? I suggest four arguments for the second concept of education, which I call *cosmopolitan education*. But first I introduce a historical digression, which traces cosmopolitanism to its origins, and in the process recover some excellent arguments that have traditionally supported it.

II

When Diogenes the Cynic replied, "I am a citizen of the world," he meant, apparently, that he refused to be defined by his local origins and group memberships, so central to the self-image of the conventional Greek male; instead, he defined himself in terms of more universal aspirations and concerns. The Stoics, who followed his lead, further developed his image of the *kosmou politês* (world citizen) arguing that each of us dwells, in effect, in two communities—the local community of our birth, and the community of human argument and aspiration that "is truly great and truly common, in which we look neither to this corner nor to that, but measure the boundaries of our nation by the sun" (Seneca, *De Otio*). It is this community that is, fundamentally, the source of our moral obligations. With respect to the most basic moral values, such as justice, "We should regard all human beings as our fellow citizens and neighbors" (Plutarch, *On the Fortunes of Alexander*). We should regard our deliberations as, first and foremost, deliberations about human problems of people in particular concrete situations, not problems growing out of a national identity that is altogether unlike that of others. Diogenes knew that the invitation to think as a world citizen was, in a sense, an invitation to be an exile from the comfort of patriotism and its easy sentiments, to see our own ways of life from the point of view of justice and the good. The accident of where one is born is just that, an accident; any human being might have been born in any nation. Recognizing this, his Stoic successors held, we should not allow differences of nationality or class or ethnic membership or even gender to erect barriers between us and our fellow human beings. We should recognize humanity wherever it occurs, and give its fundamental ingredients, reason and moral capacity, our first allegiance and respect.

This clearly did not mean that the Stoics were proposing the abolition of local and national forms of political organization and the creation of a world state. Their point was even more radical: that we should give our first allegiance to no mere form of government, no temporal power, but to the moral community made up by the humanity of all human beings. The idea of the world citizen is in this way the ancestor and the source of Kant's idea of the "kingdom of ends," and has a similar function in inspiring and regulating moral and political conduct. One should always behave so as to treat with equal respect the dignity of reason and moral choice in every human being. It is this concept that also inspires Tagore's novel, as the cosmopolitan landlord struggles to stem the tide of nationalism and factionalism by appeals to universal moral norms. Many of the speeches of the character Nikhil were drawn from Tagore's own cosmopolitan political writings.

Stoics who hold that good civic education is education for world citizenship recommend this attitude on three grounds. First, they hold that the study of humanity as it is realized in the whole world is valuable for self-knowledge: we see ourselves more clearly when we see our ways in relation to those of other reasonable people.

Second, they argue, as does Tagore, that we will be better able to solve our problems if we face them in this way. No theme is deeper in Stoicism than the damage done by faction and local allegiances to the political life of a group. Political deliberation, they argue, is sabotaged again and again by partisan loyalties, whether to one's team at the Circus or to one's nation. Only by making our fundamental allegiance to the world community of justice and reason do we avoid these dangers.

Finally, they insist that the stance of the *kosmou politês* is intrinsically valuable, for it recognizes in people what is especially fundamental about them, most worthy of respect and acknowledgment: their aspirations to justice and goodness and their capacities for reasoning in this connection. These qualities may be less colorful than local or national traditions and identities—it is on this basis that the young wife in Tagore's novel spurns them in favor of qualities in the nationalist orator Sandip that she later comes to see as superficial—but they are, the Stoics argue, both lasting and deep.

The Stoics stress that to be a citizen of the world one does not need to give up local identifications, which can be a source of great richness in life. They suggest that we think of ourselves not as devoid of local affiliations, but as surrounded by a series of concentric circles. The first one encircles the self, the next takes in the immediate family, then follows the extended family, then, in order, neighbors or local groups, fellow city-dwellers, and fellow countrymen—and we can easily add to this list groupings based on ethnic, linguistic, historical, professional, gender, or sexual identities. Outside all these circles is the largest one, humanity as a whole. Our task as citizens of the world will be to "draw the circles somehow toward the center" (Stoic philosopher Hierocles, 1st–2nd CE), making all human beings more like our fellow city-dwellers, and so on. We need not give up our special affections and identifications, whether ethnic or gender-based or religious. We need not think of them as superficial, and we may think of our identity as constituted partly by them. We may and should devote special attention to them in education. But we should also work to make all human beings part of our community of dialogue and concern, base our political deliberations on that interlocking commonality, and give the circle that defines our humanity special attention and respect.

In educational terms, this means that students in the United States, for example, may continue to regard themselves as defined partly by their particular loves—their families, their religious, ethnic, or racial communities, or even their country. But they must also, and centrally, learn to recognize humanity wherever they encounter it, undeterred by traits that are strange to them, and be eager to understand humanity in all its strange guises. They must learn enough about the different to recognize common aims, aspirations, and values, and enough about these common ends to see how variously they are instantiated in the many cultures and their histories. Stoic writers insist that the vivid imagining of the different is an essential task of education, and that it requires, in turn, a mastery of many facts about the different. Marcus Aurelius gives himself the following advice, which might be called the basis for cosmopolitan education: "Accustom yourself not to be inattentive to what another person says, and as far as possible enter into that person's mind" (VI. 53). "Generally," he adds, "one must first learn many things before one can judge another's action with understanding."

A favored exercise in this process of world thinking is to conceive of the entire world of human beings as a single body, its many people as so many limbs. Referring to the fact that it takes only changing a single letter in Greek to convert the word "limb" (*melos*) into the word "part" (*meros*), Marcus says: "If, changing the word, you call yourself merely a [detached] part rather than a limb, you do not yet love your fellow men from the heart, nor derive complete joy from doing good; you will do it merely as a duty, not as doing good to yourself" (VII. 13). It is important to recall that, as emperor, he gave himself that advice in connection with daily duties that required coming to grips with the cultures of remote and, initially, strange civilizations, such as Parthia and Sarmatia.

I would like to see education adopt this cosmopolitan Stoic stance. The organic model could, of course, be abused—if, for example, it was taken to deny the fundamental importance of the separateness of people and of fundamental personal liberties. Stoics were not always sufficiently attentive to these values and to their political salience; in that sense, their thought is not always a good basis for a scheme of democratic deliberation and education. But as the image is primarily intended—as a reminder of the interdependence of all human beings and communities—it has fundamental significance. There is clearly a huge amount to be said about how such ideas might be realized in curricula at many levels. Instead of beginning that more concrete task, however, I focus on the present day and offer four arguments for making world citizenship, rather than democratic or national citizenship, the focus for civic education.

III

*1. Through cosmopolitan education, we learn more
about ourselves.*

One of the greatest barriers to rational deliberation in politics is the unexamined feeling that one's own preferences and ways are neutral and natural. An education that takes national boundaries as morally salient too often reinforces this kind of irrationality, by lending to what is an accident of history a false air of moral weight and glory. By looking at ourselves through the lens of the other, we come to see what in our practices is local and nonessential, what is more broadly or deeply shared. Our nation is appallingly ignorant of most of the rest of the world. I think this means that it is also, in many crucial ways, ignorant of itself.

To give just one example of this: If we want to understand our own history and our choices about child-rearing and the structure of the family, we are helped immeasurably by looking around the world to see in what configurations families exist, and through what strategies children are in fact being cared for. (This would include a study of the history of the family, both in our own and other traditions.) Such a study can show us, for example, that the two-parent nuclear family, in which the mother is the primary homemaker and the father the primary breadwinner, is by no means a pervasive style of child-rearing in today's world. The extended family, clusters of families, the village, women's associations—all these groups, and others, in various places in the world have major child-rearing responsibilities. Seeing this, we can begin to ask questions—for example, about how much child abuse there is in a family that involves grandparents and other relatives in child-rearing, as compared with the relatively isolated Western-style nuclear family; or about how the different structures of child care support women's work.[4] If we do not undertake this kind of educational project, we risk assuming that the options familiar to us are the only ones there are, and that they are somehow "normal" and "natural" for all humans. Much the same can be said about conceptions of gender and sexuality, about conceptions of work and its division, about schemes of property holding, or about the treatment of children and the aged.

2. We make headway solving problems that require international cooperation.

The air does not obey national boundaries. This simple fact can be, for children, the beginning of the recognition that, like it or not, we live in a world in which the destinies of nations are closely intertwined with respect to basic goods and survival itself. The pollution of third-world nations that are attempting to attain our high standard of living will, in some cases, end up in our air. No matter what account of these matters we will finally adopt, any intelligent deliberation about ecology—as, also, about the food supply and population—requires global planning, global knowledge, and the recognition of a shared future.

To conduct this sort of global dialogue, we need knowledge not only of the geography and ecology of other nations—something that would already entail much revision in our curricula—but also a great deal about their people, so that in talking with them we may be capable of respecting their traditions and commitments. Cosmopolitan education would supply the background necessary for this type of deliberation.

3. We recognize moral obligations to the rest of the world that are real and that otherwise would go unrecognized.

What are Americans to make of the fact that the high living standard we enjoy is one that very likely cannot be universalized, at least given the present costs of pollution controls and the present economic situation of developing nations, without ecological disaster? If we take Kantian morality at all seriously, as we should, we need to educate our children to be troubled by this fact. Otherwise we are educating a nation of moral hypocrites who talk the language of universalizability but whose universe has a self-serving, narrow scope.

This point may appear to presuppose universalism, rather than being an argument in its favor. But here one may note that the values on which Americans may most justly pride themselves are, in a deep sense, Stoic values: respect for human dignity and the opportunity for each person to pursue happiness. If we really do believe that all human beings are created equal and endowed with certain inalienable rights, we are morally required to think about what that conception requires us to do with and for the rest of the world.

Once again, that does not mean that one may not permissibly give one's own sphere a special degree of concern. Politics, like child care, will be poorly done if each thinks herself equally responsible for all, rather than giving the immediate surroundings special attention and care. To give one's own sphere special care is justifiable in universalist terms, and I think this is its most compelling justification. To take one example, we do not really think our own children are morally more important than other people's children, even though almost all of us who have children would give our own children far more love and care than we give others'. It is good for children, on the whole, that things work this way, and that is why our special care is good, rather than selfish. Education may and should reflect those special concerns—for example, in a given nation, spending more time on that nation's history and politics. But my argument does entail the idea that we should not confine our thinking to our own sphere, that in making choices in both political and economic matters we should most seriously consider the right of other human beings to life, liberty, and the pursuit of happiness, and that we should work to acquire the knowledge that will enable us to deliberate well about those rights. I believe this sort of thinking will have large-scale economic and political consequences.

4. We make a consistent and coherent argument based on distinctions we are prepared to defend.

In Richard Rorty's and Sheldon Hackney's eloquent appeals to shared values, there is something that makes me very uneasy. They seem to argue effectively when they insist on the centrality to democratic deliberation of certain values that bind all citizens together. But why should these values, which instruct us to join hands across boundaries of ethnicity, class, gender, and race, lose steam when they get to the borders of the nation? By conceding that a morally arbitrary boundary such as the boundary of the nation has a deep and formative role in our deliberations, we seem to deprive ourselves of any principled way of persuading citizens they should in fact join hands across these other barriers.

For one thing, the very same groups exist both outside and inside. Why should we think of people from China as our fellows the minute they dwell in a certain place, namely the United States, but not when they dwell in a certain other place, namely China? What is it about the national boundary that magically converts people toward whom we are both incurious and indifferent into people to whom we have duties of mutual respect? I think, in short, that we undercut the very case for multicultural respect within a nation by failing to make central to education a broader world respect. Richard Rorty's patriotism may be a way of bringing all Americans together; but patriotism is very close to jingoism, and I'm afraid I don't see in Rorty's argument any proposal for coping with this very obvious danger.

Furthermore, the defense of shared national values in both Rorty and Hackney, as I understand it, requires appealing to certain basic features of human personhood that obviously also transcend national boundaries. So if we fail to educate children to cross those boundaries in their minds and imaginations, we are tacitly giving them the message that we don't really mean what we say. We say that respect should be accorded to humanity as such, but we really mean that Americans as such are worthy of special respect. And that, I think, is a story that Americans have told for far too long.

IV

Becoming a citizen of the world is often a lonely business. It is, as Diogenes said, a kind of exile—from the comfort of local truths, from the warm, nestling feeling of patriotism, from the absorbing drama of pride in oneself and one's own. In the writings of Marcus Aurelius (as in those of his American followers Emerson and Thoreau), a reader can sometimes sense a boundless loneliness, as if the removal of the props of habit and local boundaries had left life bereft of any warmth or security. If one begins life as a child who loves and trusts his or her parents, it is tempting to want to reconstruct citizenship along the same lines, finding in an idealized image of a nation a surrogate parent who will do one's thinking for one. Cosmopolitanism offers no such refuge; it offers only reason and the love of humanity, which may seem at times less colorful than other sources of belonging.

In Tagore's novel, the appeal to world citizenship fails. It fails because patriotism is full of color and intensity and passion, whereas cosmopolitanism seems to have a hard time gripping the imagination. And yet in its very failure, Tagore shows, it succeeds. For the novel is a story of education for world citizenship, since the entire tragic story is told by the widowed Bimala, who understands, if too late, that Nikhil's morality was vastly superior to Sandip's empty symbol-mongering, that what looked like passion in Sandip was egocentric self-exaltation, and that what looked like lack of passion in Nikhil contained a truly loving perception of her as a person. If one goes today to Santiniketan, a town several hours by train from Calcutta where Tagore founded his cosmopolitan university, Vishvabharati (which means "all the world")—one feels the tragedy once more. For all-the-world university has not achieved the anticipated influence or distinction within India, and the ideals of the cosmopolitan community of Santiniketan are increasingly under siege from militant forces of ethnocentric particularism and Hindu-fundamentalist nationalism. And yet, in the very decline of Tagore's ideal, which now threatens the very existence of the secular and tolerant Indian state, the observer sees its worth. To worship one's country as if it were a god is indeed to bring a curse upon it. Recent electoral reactions against Hindu nationalism give some grounds for optimism that this recognition of worth is widespread and may prove efficacious, averting a tragic ending of the sort that Tagore describes.

And since I am in fact optimistic that Tagore's ideal can be successfully realized in schools and universities in democracies around the world, and in the formation of public policy, let me conclude with a story of cosmopolitanism that has a happy ending. It is told by Diogenes Laertius about the courtship and marriage of the Cynic cosmopolitan philosophers Crates and Hipparchia (one of the most eminent female philosophers of antiquity), in order, presumably, to show that casting off the symbols of status and nation can sometimes be a way to succeed in love. The background is that Hipparchia is from a good family, attached, as most Greek families were, to social status and pedigree. They resent the cosmopolitan philosopher Crates, with his strange ideas of world citizenship and his strange disdain for rank and boundaries.

> [Hipparchia] fell in love with Crates' arguments and his way of life and paid no attention to any of her suitors nor to wealth or high birth or good looks. Crates, though, was everything to her. Moreover, she

told her parents that she would kill herself if she were not married off to him. So Crates was called on by her parents to talk their daughter out of it; he did all he could, but in the end he didn't persuade her. So he stood up and threw off his clothes in front of her and said, "Here is your bridegroom; these are his possessions; make your decision accordingly—for you cannot be my companion unless you undertake the same way of life." The girl chose him. Adopting the same clothing and style of life she went around with her husband and they copulated in public and they went off together to dinner parties. And once she went to a dinner party at the house of Lysimachus and there refuted Theodorus the Atheist, with a sophism like this: "If it wouldn't be judged wrong for Theodorus to do something, then it wouldn't be judged wrong for Hipparchia to do it either; but Theodorus does no wrong if he beats himself; so Hipparchia too does no wrong if she beats Theodorus." And when Theodorus could not reply to her argument, he ripped off her cloak. But Hipparchia was not upset or distraught as a woman would normally be. (DL 6.96-8)[5]

I am not exactly recommending Crates and Hipparchia as the marital ideal for students in my hypothetical cosmopolitan schools (or Theodorus the Atheist as their logic teacher).[6] But the story does reveal this: that the life of the cosmopolitan, who puts right before country and universal reason before the symbols of national belonging, need not be boring, flat, or lacking in love.

II

Kwame Anthony Appiah
Cosmopolitan Patriots

My father was a Ghanaian patriot. He once published a column in the *Pioneer*, our local newspaper in Kumasi, under the headline "Is Ghana worth dying for?" and it was clear that his answer was yes.[1] But he also loved Asante—the region of Ghana where he and I both grew up—a kingdom absorbed within a British colony, then also a region of a new multiethnic Republic, a kingdom he and his father had also once loved and served. And, like so many African nationalists of his class and generation, he always loved an enchanting abstraction they called "Africa."

When he died, my sisters and I found a note he had drafted and never quite finished, last words of love and wisdom for his children. After a few paragraphs reminding us of our double ancestry, in Ghana and in England, he wrote: "Remember that you are citizens of the world." And he went on to tell us that this meant that wherever we chose to live—as citizens of the world we could surely choose to live anywhere—we should make sure we left that place better than we found it. "Deep inside of me," he went on, "is a great love for mankind and an abiding desire to see mankind, under God, fulfill its highest destiny."

The favorite slander of the narrow nationalist against us cosmopolitans is that we are rootless: What my father believed in, however, was a rooted cosmopolitanism, or, if you like, a cosmopolitan patriotism. Like Gertrude Stein, he thought there was no point in roots if you couldn't take them with you. "America is my country and Paris is my hometown," Stein said.[2] My father would have understood her.

Some might complain that cosmopolitanism must be parasitic: Where, they will ask, would Stein have gotten her roots in a fully cosmopolitan world? Where, in other words, would all the diversity we cosmopolitans celebrate come from in a world where there were only cosmopolitans?

The answer is straightforward: The cosmopolitan patriot can entertain the possibility of a world in which everyone is a rooted cosmopolitan, attached to a home of his or her own, with its own cultural particularities, but taking pleasure from the presence of other, different, places that are home to other, different, people. The cosmopolitan also imagines that in such a world not everyone will find it best to stay in their natal patria, so that the circulation of people between different localities will involve not only cultural tourism (which the cosmopolitan admits to enjoying) but migration, nomadism, diaspora. (In the past, these processes have usually been the result of forces we should deplore: the old migrants were often refugees, and older diasporas often began in an involuntary exile. But what can be hateful if coerced can be celebrated when it flows from the free decisions of individuals or groups.)

In a world of cosmopolitan patriots, people would accept the citizen's responsibility to nurture the culture and politics of their homes. Many would, no doubt, spend their lives in the places that shaped them; and that is one of the reasons local cultural practices would be sustained and transmitted. But many would move, and that would mean that cultural practices would travel also (as they have always traveled). The result would be a world in which each local form of human life was the result of long term and persistent processes of cultural hybridization: a world, in that respect, much like the world we live in now.

Behind the objection that cosmopolitanism is parasitic is, in any case, an anxiety that we should dispel: an exaggerated estimate of the rate of disappearance of cultural heterogeneity. In the global system of cultural exchanges, some forms of human life are disappearing, and the processes of homogenization are somewhat asymmetrical. Neither of these phenomena are particularly new, but their range and speed probably are. Nevertheless, as forms of culture disappear, new forms are created, and they are created locally, which means they have exactly the regional inflections that cosmopolitans celebrate. The disappearance of old cultural forms is, in short, consistent with a rich variety of forms of human life, just because new cultural forms that differ from each other are also being created all the time.

Cosmopolitanism and patriotism, unlike nationalism, are sentiments more than ideologies. Different political ideologies can be made consistent with both. Some cosmopolitan patriots are conservative and religious; others are secularizers of a socialist bent. Christian cosmopolitanism is as old as the merger with the Roman Empire, through which Stoicism came to be a dominant shaping force in Christian ethics. (On my father's bedside were Cicero and the Bible. Only someone ignorant of the history of the church would see this as an expression of divided loyalties.) But I am a liberal, and both cosmopolitanism and patriotism, as sentiments, can seem to be hard to accommodate to liberal principles.

Patriotism often challenges liberalism. Liberals who propose a state that does not take sides in the debates among its citizens' various conceptions of the good are held to be unable to value a state that celebrates itself—and modern self-described patriots (here in

America, at least) often desire a public education and a public culture that stoke the fires of the national ego. Patriots also seem especially sensitive these days to slights to the national honor, to skepticism about a celebratory nationalist historiography—in short, to the critical reflection on the state that we liberals, with our instrumental conception of it, are bound to engage in. No liberal should say "My country, right or wrong," because liberalism involves a set of political principles that a state can fail to realize; and the liberal will have no special loyalty to an illiberal state, because liberals value people over collectivities.

This patriotic objection to liberalism can also be made, however, to Catholicism, to Islam, to almost any religious view; indeed, to any view, including humanism, that claims a higher moral authority than one's own particular political community. And the answer to it is to affirm, first, that someone who loves principle can also love country, family, friends; and second, that a true patriot holds the state and the community within which she lives to certain standards, has moral aspirations for them, and that those aspirations may be liberal.

The cosmopolitan challenge to liberalism begins with the claim that liberals have been too preoccupied with morality *within* the nation-state. John Rawls's *Theory of Justice*, which began the modern reformulation of philosophical liberalism, left the questions of international morality to be dealt with later. How to develop the Rawlsian picture in an international direction is a current preoccupation of professional political philosophy. The cosmopolitan is likely to argue that this order of priorities is all wrong.

It is all very well to argue for or fight for liberalism in your own country. But if that country, in its international operations, supports, or even tolerates, illiberal regimes elsewhere, then it fails, the cosmopolitan will argue, because it does not sufficiently weigh the lives of human beings as such. Liberals take it to be self-evident that we are all "created equal" and that we bear certain "inalienable rights,"[3] and then seem almost immediately to become preoccupied with looking after the rights of the local branch of the species, forgetting—this is the cosmopolitan critique—that their rights matter as human rights and thus matter only if the rights of foreign humans matter, too.

This is surely more of an objection to the practice of liberalism than to its theory (and, as I shall argue later, cosmopolitans also have a reason for caring about states). At the heart of the liberal picture of humanity is the idea of the equal dignity of all persons: Liberalism grows with an increasing appreciation of the inadequacy of an older picture in which dignity was the possession of an elite. Not every premodern society made its elite hereditary, as the eunuchs who ran the Ottoman Empire would have attested. But it is only in the modern age that the idea has grown that every one of us begins life with an equal entitlement to respect: an entitlement that we may, perhaps, lose through misbehavior, but which otherwise remains with us all our lives.

This idea of the equal dignity of all persons can be cashed out in different ways, but it is what undergirds the attachment to a democracy of unlimited franchise; the renunciation of sexism and racism and heterosexism; the respect for the autonomy of individuals, which resists the state's desire to fit us to someone else's conception of what is good for us; and the notion of human rights—rights possessed by human beings as such—that is at the heart of liberal theory.

It would be wrong, however, to conflate cosmopolitanism and humanism; wrong, because cosmopolitanism is not just the feeling that everybody matters. The cosmopolitan also celebrates the fact that there are different local human ways of being, while humanism is consistent with the desire for global homogeneity. Humanism can be made compatible with cosmopolitan sentiments, but it can also live with a deadening urge to uniformity.

A liberal cosmopolitanism of the sort I am defending might put its point like this: We value the variety of human forms of social and cultural life, we do not want everybody to become part of a homogeneous global culture, and we know that this means that there will also be local differences (both within and between states) in moral climate. So long as these differences meet certain general ethical constraints—so long, in particular, as political institutions respect basic human rights—we are happy to let them be.

PATRIOTISM, AS COMMUNITARIANS HAVE SPENT MUCH time reminding us recently, is about the responsibilities as well as the privileges of citizenship. But it is also, and above all, not so much a matter of action—of practical morality—as of sentiment: If there is one emotion that *patriotism* brings to mind, it is surely pride. When the national anthem plays, when the national team wins, when the national army prevails, there is that shiver down the spine, the electric excitement, the thrill of being on the winning side. But the patriot is surely also the first to suffer his or her country's shame: it is the patriot who suffers when a country elects the wrong leaders, or when those leaders prevaricate, bluster, pantomime, or betray "our" principles. Patriotism is about what the nineteenth-century Liberian scholar-diplomat Edward Blyden once so memorably called "the poetry of politics," which is the feeling of "people with whom we are connected."[4] It is the connection and sentiment that matter, and there is no reason to suppose that everybody in this complex, ever-mutating world will find their affinities and their passions focused on a single place.

My father's example demonstrates for me, more clearly than any abstract argument, the possibilities that the enemies of cosmopolitanism deny. We cosmopolitans *can* be patriots, loving our homelands (not only the states where we were born but the states where we grew up and where we live). Our loyalty to humankind—so vast, so abstract, a unity—does not deprive us of the capacity to care for people closer by; the notion of a global citizenship can have a real and practical meaning.

But my father's example makes me suspicious of the purportedly cosmopolitan argument against patriotism (my father's Ghanaian patriotism, which I want to defend) that alleges that nationality is, in the words of Martha Nussbaum in her fine essay, "a morally irrelevant characteristic." Nussbaum argues that in "conceding that a morally arbitrary boundary such as the boundary of the nation has a deep and formative role in our deliberations, we seem to deprive ourselves of any principled way of persuading citizens that they should in fact join hands" across the "boundaries of ethnicity and class and gender and race."

I can only say what I think is wrong here if I insist on the distinction between state and nation.[5] Their conflation is a perfectly natural one for a modern person—even after Rwanda, Sri Lanka, Amritsar, Bosnia, and Azerbaijan. But the yoking of nation and state in the Enlightenment was intended to bring the arbitrary boundaries of states into conformity with the "natural" boundaries of nations; the idea that the boundaries of one could be arbitrary while the boundaries of the other were not is easy enough to grasp, once we are reminded of it.

Not that I want to endorse this essentially Herderian way of thinking—Nations never preexist states. Loosely and unphilosophically defined, a nation is an "imagined community" of culture or ancestry running beyond the scale of the face-to-face and seeking political expression.[6] But all the nations I can think of that are not coterminous with states are the legacy of older state arrangements—as Asante is in what has become Ghana, and as the Serbian and Croatian nations are in what used to be Yugoslavia.

I want, in fact, to distinguish the nation and the state to make a point entirely opposite to Herder's: If anything is morally arbitrary, it is not the state but the nation.[7] Since human beings live in political orders narrower than the species, and since it is within those political orders that questions of public right and wrong are largely argued out and decided, the fact of being a fellow-citizen—someone who is a member of the same order—is not morally arbitrary at all. That is why the cosmopolitan critique of liberalism's focus on the state is overstated: because the cultural variability that cosmopolitanism celebrates has come to depend on the existence of a plurality of states, we need to take states seriously.

The nation, on the other hand, *is* arbitrary, but not in a way that permits us to discard it in our moral reflections. It is arbitrary in the root sense of that term, because it is, according to the *Oxford English Dictionary*, "dependent upon will or pleasure." Nations often matter more to people than states: Monoethnic Serbia makes more sense to some than multicultural Bosnia; a Hutu or a Tutsi Rwanda makes more sense to others than a peaceful shared citizenship of Tutsi and Hutu; only when Britain or France became nations as well as states did ordinary citizens come to care much about being French or British. But notice that the reason nations matter is that they matter to *people*. Nations matter morally, when they do, in other words, for the same reason that football and opera matter—as things desired by autonomous agents, whose autonomous desires we ought to acknowledge and take account of even if we cannot always accede to them.

States, on the other hand, matter morally intrinsically. They matter not because people care about them, but because they regulate our lives through forms of coercion that will always require moral justification. State institutions matter because they are both necessary to so many modern human purposes and because they have so great a potential for abuse. As Hobbes saw, to do its job the state has to have a monopoly of certain forms of authorized coercion, and the exercise of that authority cries out for (but often does not deserve) justification even in places, like so many post-colonial societies, where many people have no positive feeling for the state at all.

There is, then, no need for the cosmopolitan to claim that the state is morally arbitrary in the way that I have suggested the nation is. There are many reasons to think that living in political communities narrower than the species is better for us than would be our engulfment in a single world-state, a cosmopolis of which we cosmopolitans would be not figurative but literal citizens. It is, in fact, precisely this celebration of cultural variety that distinguishes the cosmopolitan from some of the other heirs of Enlightenment humanism.

It is because humans live best on a smaller scale that we should defend not just the state, but the county, the town, the street, the business, the craft, the profession, and the family, as communities, as circles among the many circles that are narrower than the human horizon, that are appropriate spheres of moral concern. We should, as cosmopolitans, defend the right of others to live in democratic states with rich possibilities of association within and across their borders, states of which they can be patriotic citizens. And, as cosmopolitans, we can claim that right for ourselves.

Benjamin R. Barber
Constitutional Faith

WRITING IN THE GREAT TRADITION OF KANT
and the Stoics, Martha Nussbaum deploys the noble
ideal of cosmopolitanism against the manifold parochi-
alisms of patriotism, nationalism, and ethnicity. She is
especially unhappy with recent American attempts at
adducing a national identity because they risk substituting a "colorful idol for the substantive values of justice
and right." She wants us to emulate Tagore's Nikhil and
resist the temptations of an American *Bande Mataram*.

I have two problems with Nussbaum's admirable exercise in Kantian universalism. First, she underappreci-
ates the success of the American experiment in grafting
the sentiments of patriotism onto a constitutional frame
defined precisely by the "substantive values of justice
and right" she prizes. And second, she underestimates
the thinness of cosmopolitanism and the crucial hu-
manizing role played by identity politics in a deracinat-
ing world of contracts, markets, and legal personhood.
Patriotism has its pathologies, but so does cosmopolitanism. Because she misjudges these two elements, she

is unduly alarmed about what has been a remarkably successful and undogmatic constitutional exercise in American exceptionalism and unduly frightened of efforts to refocus American patriotism and community in an era of individualism and privatizing markets. In an overly tribalized world, cosmopolitanism might be a useful counterpoint. But ours is a world disenchanted in which *Gemeinschaft* and neighborhood have for the most part been supplanted by *Gesellschaft* and bureaucracy. What we require are healthy, democratic forms of local community and civic patriotism rather than abstract universalism and the thin gruel of contract relations.

AMERICAN NATIONAL IDENTITY HAS FROM THE START been a remarkable mixture of cosmopolitanism and parochialism. The colonists and later the founders understood themselves to be engaged in a novel process of uprooting and rerooting. In his celebrated *Letters from an American Farmer*, St. John Crevecoeur sets the tone for America's new form of patriotism, conceived precisely to counter the religious parochialism and persecutions from which immigrants to America were fleeing. American patriotism was itself the counter to the very evils Nussbaum associates with American patriotism. Crevecoeur solemnizes the creation of a "new man" in "the great American asylum [where] . . . everything tended to regenerate [men] . . . new laws, a new mode of living, a new social system: here they are become men; in Europe they were so many useless plants . . . [here] they have taken root and flourished." How has that happened? "By what power hath this surprising metamorphosis been performed? By that of the laws." American civic identity is invented to bar the confessional wars Nussbaum fears it will occasion.

Jefferson himself echoes Crevecoeur when he writes, "Let this be the distinctive mark of an American, that in cases of commotion he enlists under no man's banner, but repairs to the standard of the law." And just a few years later the feisty English emigrant Frances Wright, herself unable to vote, nonetheless joined in celebrating the new American patriotism, seeming to remonstrate explicitly with Nussbaum: "What is it to be an American?" Wright asks. "Is it to have drawn the first breath in Maine, in Pennsylvania, in Florida, or in Missouri? Pshaw! Hence with such paltry, pettifogging calculations of nativities! They are Americans who have complied with the constitutional regulations of the United States. . . . wed the principles of America's declaration to their hearts and render the duties of American citizens practically to their lives." Still more recently, Justice Felix Frankfurter spoke of the need "to shed old loyalties and take on the loyalty of American citizenship," which is a kind of "fellowship which binds people together by devotion to certain feelings and ideas and ideals summarized as a requirement that they be attached to the principles of the constitution."

Elsewhere, I have tried to sum up this approach to Americanism by suggesting that "from the outset, then, to be an American was also to be enmeshed in a unique story of freedom, to be free (or to be enslaved) in a novel sense, more existential than political or legal. Even in colonial times, the new world meant starting over again, meant freedom from rigid and heavily freighted traditional cultures. Deracination was the universal experience. . . . To be an American was not to acquire a new race or a new religion or a new culture, it was to possess a new set of political ideas" (*An Aristocracy of Everyone*).

The American trick was to use the fierce attachments of patriotic sentiment to bond a people to high ideals. Our "tribal" sources from which we derive our sense of national identity are the Declaration of Independence, the Constitution and the Bill of Rights, the inaugural addresses of our presidents, Lincoln's Gettysburg Address, and Martin Luther King's "free at last" sermon at the 1963 March on Washington—not so much the documents themselves as the felt sentiments tying us to them, sentiments that are rehearsed at Independence Day parades and in Memorial Day speeches. If Sheldon Hackney wants to recreate a sense of such patriotic rhetoric among ordinary Americans, he surely is more likely to strengthen than to imperil the civic fabric and the American commitment to cosmopolitan ideals.

At times, Nussbaum seems to come close to recognizing as much, acknowledging that even among cosmopolitans the circles must be drawn toward the center. But she is distrustful, worrying that in the end patriotism, however conceived, is "close to jingoism." She seems diffident in the face of the actual ideals that animate American patriotism—however little realized they may be. Yet it is precisely these ideals that give parochial America its global appeal, these ideals that afforded Lincoln the opportunity to claim that America might yet be the "last best hope" for people everywhere, these ideals that draw peoples damaged by toxic patriotisms elsewhere to American shores. Justice Hugo Black captured America's patriotic idealism in the phrase "constitutional faith." More recently, Sanford Levinson wrote a lively testament to Black's idea—also called *Constitutional Faith*. At its best (it often is not at its best), America's civic nativism is, then, a celebration of internationalism, a devotion to values with cosmopolitan reach. The cosmopolitanization of such values has even gotten America in trouble (in Mexico under Wilson, in Vietnam under Kennedy, Johnson, and Nixon, and perhaps now in Bosnia)—a reminder to Nussbaum that cosmopolitanism too has its pathologies and can also breed its own antiseptic version of imperialism.

My second objection to Nussbaum's worries is that, though she is not entirely unmindful of the problem, she finally understates the thinness of cosmopolitanism. Like such kindred ideas as legal personhood, contract society, and the economic market, the idea of cosmopolitanism offers little or nothing for the human psyche to fasten on. By her own admission, it "seems to have a hard time gripping the imagination." Not just the imagination: the heart, the viscera, the vitals of the body that houses the brain in which Nussbaum would like us to dwell. No one actually lives "in the world of which the cosmopolitan wishes us to be good citizens." Rather, we live in this particular neighborhood of the world, that block, this valley, that seashore, this family. Our attachments start parochially and only then grow outward. To bypass them in favor of an immediate cosmopolitanism is to risk ending up nowhere—feeling at home neither at home nor in the world. This is the lesson of America's tempestuous multicultural politics: to become an American, women and men must first identify as African Americans or Polish Americans or Jewish Americans or German Americans; to acquire the dignity of natural citizens they must first take pride in their local communities. Diogenes may have regarded himself a citizen of the world, but global citizenship demands of its patriots levels of abstraction and disembodiment most women and men will be unable or unwilling to muster, at least in the first instance.

Like Ibsen's Pastor Brand, Nussbaum urges her parishioners up the harsh and lonely mountain to an abstract godhead they cannot see. As ordinary women and men, they soon fall away from the quest and return to the loving warmth of their hearthsides in the valley below. Brand continues on his selfless mission, to which he has sacrificed wife, child, and parish, only to discover, too late, too late, on the mountain top, at the moment of his death, that God to whom he has given all is not the master of an abstract universe but the God of love who wants nothing more for Brand than that he love and care for those in his immediate circle down in the valley.

Nussbaum acknowledges that "becoming a citizen of the world is often a lonely business," and her mentors (Marcus Aurelius, Emerson, Thoreau) are not only solitary intellectuals who march to a different drum, but heroic figures like Brand. Nussbaum's cosmopolitanism also has something of the heroic about it, a Nietzschean quality that seems intolerant of ordinary needs and the democratic taste for the neighborhood. For the American everyman (every-woman), the representative poet is not Emerson but Whitman, not Thoreau but Woody Guthrie, bards who praised the handiwork of Lincoln and Roosevelt and who would have us travel together as comrades, drinking in the immediacy and the immensity of the American landscape, celebrating the neighborhood while urging neighbors to extend their circles of fellowship.

Nussbaum defines the cosmopolitan as a "person whose allegiance is to the worldwide community of human beings," but Whitman's allegiance is initially to the farmer, the sailor, the miner, and the shipwright. And when Guthrie sings of the American land, he sings about the specifics: "This land is your land, this land is my land, from California to the New York Island, from the redwood forest to the Gulf Stream waters . . ." Is Guthrie's rooted love of America incompatible with justice? Hardly. In nearly every song, he transmutes that love into a demand for justice. The poetry of Langston Hughes practices the same patriotic-civic alchemy when it pleads "Let America be America again," appealing not to disembodied cosmopolitanism, but to the unrealized American values that are the country's embodied soul:

O, let America be America again—
The land that never has been yet—
And yet must be—the land where everyone is free.
The land that's mine—the poor man's, Indian's Negro's, ME—

Whitman, Guthrie, and Hughes have "sung America" in a voice of loving devotion that insists the country live up to its aspirations. The old cliché has it that those who love humankind in general often cannot abide individual women or men in particular (Moliere's *Misanthrope*). Our wise American poets prudently ask us to kindle an affection for the general by reveling in the particular.

I recommend Whitman and Guthrie and Hughes to Nussbaum. They will remind her that love of homeland is not just a matter of *color*, the odd term she employs repeatedly in trying to rally a little sympathy in herself for patriots, as if she were a tourist from some black-and-white rationalist utopia touring the technicolor slums of some *National Geographic* tribal culture teeming with multihued, brightly feathered natives. But patriotism is more than color, and when it is reduced to color, the color is all too often blood-red, for it speaks to the power of the visceral human need to belong—if only by virtue of imagined identities and contrived others whose exclusion (or extermination) helps draw the boundaries.

The question is not how to do without patriotism and nationalism but how to render them safe. A civic patriotism that eschews exclusion but meets the need for parochial identity can provide an alternative to the many pathological versions of blood kinship that are around today in places like ex-Yugoslavia, Romania, Rwanda, Tajikistan, Nigeria, the Ukraine, and Afghanistan, to name just a few. I recently completed a study of this kind of fractiousness, which I subsume under the term *Jihad* (the book is called *Jihad versus McWorld*, "McWorld" being my name for the toxic cosmopolitanism of global markets). But Jihad is a sickness of the national body and cannot be treated with remedies aimed at detaching the soul from it. Pathological patriotism can be cured only by healthy patriotism, jingoism only by a pacific constitutional faith, destructive nationalism only by liberal nationalism (in the title of Yael Tamir's book), separatist, exclusionary ethnicity only by multicultural ethnicity. If the tribes of traditional community are dangerous, then we need to find forms of egalitarian, democratic, and voluntarist communities that render tribalism safe. Cosmopolitanism as an attitude may help us in that effort, but cosmopolitanism as a political destination is more likely to rob us of our concreteness and our immediacy and ultimately can only benefit the less wholesome aspects of the yearning for community and identity.

Of course Nussbaum may wish to say that if, as I have argued, parochialism is the safest way to cosmopolitanism, cosmopolitanism can also be a road to parochialism. At least that is the lesson I draw from her final citation, to the noble Crates. Cosmopolitans who copulate in public and then go off to dinner parties? This is the kind of cosmopolitanism even the earthiest of parochials can understand.

Sissela Bok

From Part to Whole

AGAINST ALL FORMS OF NATIONALISM AND ethnocentrism, Martha Nussbaum challenges us to take seriously, in education as in politics, the cosmopolitan ideal that grants equal respect to all. Her essay, drawing on such thinkers as Diogenes, Marcus Aurelius, and Tagore, illuminates both what is most persuasive in this ideal and the questions it inevitably raises in practice.

Few would disagree with Nussbaum's stress on the need for greater understanding, respect, and cooperation across national and other boundaries, if societies are to mount collective responses to challenges which, themselves, respect no such boundaries—to epidemics such as AIDS, for example, or to environmental, military, and humanitarian crises. Nor would many oppose her call for children to "learn a good deal more than they frequently do about the rest of the world in which they live, about India and Bolivia and Nigeria and Norway and their histories, problems, and comparative successes."

I fully share Nussbaum's emphasis, in this regard, on aims, aspirations, and values that can be shared cross-culturally. My questions arise when she goes further, to urge that children should be taught to view themselves as citizens of the world, whose "allegiance is to the worldwide community of human beings." I am uncertain as to what children will be taught about conflicting allegiances under such a regime: whether world citizenship is to be an ideal inviting them to enlarge their perspective and to strive for broader and deeper knowledge, understanding, and care, or whether teachers must also instruct children to regard all claims to national or other identity as "morally irrelevant." In the latter case, why should they take seriously allegiances other than those to human beings in general? Why not conclude, with William Godwin, that if two persons are drowning and one is a relative of yours, then kinship (or, presumably, nationality) should make no difference in your decision as to whom to try to rescue first?

The metaphor from Hierocles that Nussbaum discusses—of concentric circles of human concern and allegiance—speaks to the necessary tensions between what we owe to insiders and outsiders of the many interlocking groups in which we find ourselves. It is a metaphor long used to urge us to stretch our concern outward from the narrowest personal confines toward the needs of outsiders, strangers, all of humanity, and sometimes also of animals, as Peter Singer proposes in *The Expanding Circle*. But more often it has been invoked to convey a contrasting view: that of "my station and its duties," according to which our allegiances depend on our situation and role in life and cannot be overridden by obligations to humanity at large.

From each of the two perspectives, the risks of misjudgment, abuse, even idolatry on the part of holders of the other perspective are seen as considerable. Nussbaum rightly points not only to the evils that we witness in so many parts of the world in the name of loyalty to kin, ethnic group, and nation, but also to the harm done by moral hypocrites who use only the language of universality. Dickens has immortalized the latter in *Martin Chuzzlewit*, in the person of Mr. Pecksniff, who cheated his fellow humans with gusto even as he intoned the language of universal love. Sometimes what is at issue is, rather, "inner hypocrisy." Thus Marcus Aurelius's inspiring reflections on cosmopolitanism, equality, and the love of one's fellow human beings did not prevent him from overseeing intensified persecution of Christians voicing those very same ideals.

From whatever perspective we view the image of the concentric circles, it conveys our ambivalence about the conflicting calls on our concern and sense of responsibility. Henry Sidgwick took the contrast between the two perspectives to be so serious as to threaten any coherent view of ethics. On one hand, he held as the fundamental principle of ethics "that another's greater good is to be preferred to one's own lesser good." According to this principle, any sacrifice on one's own part would be called for, so long as it could achieve a greater good for others, no matter where they lived.[1] On the other hand, Sidgwick also accepted what he called the common-sense view that our obligations to help others differ depending on the relationships in which we stand to them—relationships of family member, friend, neighbor, and fellow citizen.[2]

Both the universalist and the bounded view concern human survival and security. I agree with Sidgwick that neither can be dismissed out of hand as morally irrelevant. Thus the duties he mentions toward family members are ones known, in some form, to every society and moral tradition: without some internal support and loyalty, no group, however small, could survive. Holders of both views may concur on the survival value of at least a few such duties, even as they disagree on the extent to which narrower duties should be allowed to conflict with duties to humanity at large. At the same time, many exponents of both views concede that certain prohibitions, as on killing, breaking promises, and cheating, ought to hold across all the boundaries of all the circles, and that in certain acute emergencies—after an earthquake, for example—the obligation to offer humanitarian aid across boundaries may supersede domestic needs.

Apart from such limited areas of agreement, however, the two perspectives lead to glaringly different conclusions about domestic and international policy. When the needs of outsiders, however defined, are of vast extent and prolonged duration and would require a considerable reallocation of scarce resources, holders of the bounded view are especially likely to refuse to grant priority to such needs over those of family members or compatriots.

We see the two perspectives invoked with passion in current debates about immigration, foreign aid, and humanitarian intervention. As the gap between the haves and have-nots widens, within societies and internationally, the differences between the two take on ever sharper practical import. The world's population has expanded over six times since Sidgwick contrasted the universalist and the more bounded views of human responsibility and noted the threat that the reasonableness of both posed for ethics. The 1.3 billion persons who now live in extreme need—many of them children, many unable to survive without outside help—are more numerous than all human beings who lived in his time. This vast expansion of human misery is paralleled, however, by even greater growth in the numbers of the well-to-do. Even as global levels of average longevity, nutrition, health, and literacy continue to climb, the gap only widens between rich and poor: Just in the last three decades, the income gap between the world's richest 20 percent and poorest 20 percent has doubled.

This widening gap between haves and have-nots, and the sheer magnitude and intensity of present suffering, challenge, I suggest, all existing conceptions of human rights and duties and obligations. What does it require in practice, under today's conditions, to give priority either to world citizenship or to national or community allegiances? What does it mean to honor human rights or to take seriously the duty to aid fellow humans in distress? And whose obligation is it to offer assistance on the scale now needed, or to protect rights, such as those not to be killed or tortured, when violated by others abroad?

These questions trouble many cosmopolitan and noncosmopolitan thinkers and human rights activists alike and will form the background for policy debates in the century to come. Nussbaum's essay helps to clarify the conflicts at issue; and the metaphor of concentric circles to which she refers encourages participants in such debates to envisage problems both from within and without the different circles, and, more generally, from the two discrepant perspectives on them to which Sidgwick points.

The two perspectives, therefore, also matter for debates about educational approaches to enable children to better reflect on the range of their allegiances. I see no reason to teach children that claims to national or other identities are "morally irrelevant." Rather, the question is how, and on what grounds, to weigh these claims when they conflict, and what responsibility to acknowledge with respect to each. Educational programs that declare either a global or a more bounded perspective to be the only correct one are troubling insofar as they short-circuit reflection concerning such choices.

But here a new question arises: If both perspectives are important in education, which one should be given priority, at least from the point of view of when it is first introduced? Or, to use the metaphor of the concentric circles, in which direction might children's learning about inner and outer circles and the respective allegiances best develop? Is it better for parents and teachers to begin at the outer edges and move inward, to move back and forth between the two, or to begin with the inner circles and move outward?

Alexander Pope offers one answer, in "An Essay on Man":

God loves from Whole to Parts: but human soul
Must rise from Individual to the Whole.
Self-love but serves the virtuous mind to wake,
As the small pebble stirs the peaceful lake;
The centre mov'd, a circle strait succeeds,
Another still, and still another spreads,
Friend, parent, neighbour, first it will embrace,
His country next, and next all human race,
/ . . . /

Pope's interpretation of how we learn to reach beyond the innermost circles is persuasive and worth taking into account in teaching. If children begin learning about the world "from part to whole," even as they are made familiar with the larger framework early on, they will have a basis from which to explore all they can learn about the world, and, in turn, ways of shifting back and forth between the concentric circles. They will then be better equipped to work out their stance with respect to interlocking identities, loyalties, and obligations, and to debate these with others. By contrast, children deprived of a culturally rooted education too often find it difficult to experience any allegiances whatsoever, whether to the world or to their community or family. Instead, they risk developing a debilitating sense of being exiled everywhere with responsibilities to none save themselves.

Rabindranath Tagore's philosophy of education was one, I believe, of encouraging children to reach out "from part to whole." In "A Poet's School," he describes the aims of the school he started at Santiniketan in West Bengal. Just as trees absorb nourishment from the atmosphere around them, so children, he explains, learn from "the diffuse atmosphere of culture"—one which keeps their minds sensitive to their inheritance and to the current of influences that come from tradition, and which makes it easy for them, in turn, to "imbibe the concentrated wisdom of ages."[3] But the

44 · SISSELA BOK

nourishment children draw from culture, inheritance, and tradition should be offered to them freely and thus free them to look beyond their immediate world, not constrain them through rote learning and indoctrination:

> It is only through the fullest development of all his capacities that man is likely to achieve his real freedom. He must be so equipped as no longer to be anxious about his own self-preservation; only through his capacity to understand and to sympathize with his neighbour can he function as a decent member of human society and as a responsible citizen.[4]

From such a point of view, there is nothing wrong with encouraging children fully to explore their most local existence in order to reach beyond it by degrees. Nor need there be anything wrong with lasting pride in, love for, or identification through particular bonds, communities, and cultures. Acknowledging these need not blind one to problems within any of the circles of allegiance nor involve exceptionalism or disparagement or dismissal of others. Without learning to understand the uniqueness of cultures, beginning with one's own, it may well be impossible to honor both human distinctiveness and the shared humanity central to the cosmopolitan ideal.

Judith Butler

Universality in Culture

CONSIDER THAT IT MAY BE A MISTAKE TO DE-
clare one's affiliation by stating an order of priorities: I
am X first and then Y. It may be that the ordering of
such identifications is precisely the problem produced
by a discourse on multiculturalism which does not yet
know how to relate the terms that it enumerates. It
would be a great consolation, I suppose, to return to a
ready-made universal perspective, and to compel everyone to identify with a universal moral attitude before
they take on their various specific and parochial concerns. The problem emerges, however, when the meaning of "the universal" proves to be culturally variable,
and the specific cultural articulations of the universal
work against its claim to a transcultural status.

This is not to say that there ought to be no reference
to the universal or that it has become, for us, an impos-
sibility. On the contrary. All it means is that there are
cultural conditions for its articulation that are not always the same, and that the term gains its meaning for
us precisely through these decidedly less than universal

conditions. This is a paradox that any injunction to adopt a universal attitude will encounter. For it may be that in one culture a set of rights are considered to be universally endowed, and that in another those very rights mark the limit to universalizability, i.e., "If we grant those people those rights we will be undercutting the foundations of the universal as we know it." This has become especially clear to me in the field of lesbian and gay human rights, where *the universal* is a contested term, and where various cultures and various mainstream human rights groups voice doubt over whether lesbian and gay people ought properly to be included in "the human" and whether their putative rights fit within the existing conventions governing the scope of rights considered universal.

Consider that to claim that there are existing conventions governing the scope of rights described as universal is not to claim that that scope has been decided once and for all. In fact, it may be that the universal is only partially articulated, and that we do not yet know what forms it may take. The contingent and cultural character of the existing conventions governing the scope of universality does not deny the usefulness or importance of the term *universal*. It simply means that the claim of universality has not been fully or finally made and that it remains to be seen whether and how it will be further articulated. Indeed, it may well be politically important to claim that a given set of rights are universal even when existing conventions governing the scope of universality preclude precisely such a claim. Such a claim runs the good risk of provoking a radical rearticulation of universality itself. Whether the claim is preposterous, provocative, or efficacious depends on the collective strength with which it is asserted, the institutional conditions of its assertion and reception, and the unpredictable political forces at work. But the uncertainty of success is not enough of a reason to refrain from making the claim.

Mari Matsuda has recently argued that hate speech—in particu-

lar, racially degrading speech—ought not to qualify as protected
speech precisely because it sends a message of racial inferiority,
and that message has been refuted by universally accepted codes of
law.[1] Setting aside for the moment whether or not hate speech
ought to be unprotected for that reason, the argument raises other
kinds of questions. Is Matsuda's view one which only isolates
kinds of speech that ought not to be part of public discourse, or is
it also a normative position concerning what ought to be the positive boundaries of legitimate speech—namely, speech that is con-
strained by *existing* notions of universality?[2] How would we reconcile such a view with that of Étienne Balibar, for instance, who
argues that racism informs our current notions of universality?[3]
How might we continue to insist upon more expansive reformula-
tions of universality, if we commit ourselves to honoring only the
provisional and parochial versions of universality currently encoded in international law? Clearly, such precedents are enor-
mously useful for political arguments in international contexts, but
it would be a mistake to think that such conventional formulations
exhaust the possibilities of what might be meant by "the universal." Are we to expect that we will know in advance the meaning to
be assigned to the utterance of universality, or is this utterance the
occasion for a meaning that is not to be fully or concretely anticipated?

If standards of universality are historically articulated, then it
would seem that exposing the parochial and exclusionary character of a given historical articulation of universality is part of the
project of extending and rendering substantive the notion of universality itself. "Speech that contests current standards governing
the universal reach of political enfranchisement" characterizes racist speech, to be sure. But there are other sorts of speech that constitute valuable contestations crucial to the continuing elaboration
of the universal itself, and which it would be a mistake to foreclose.
An example of the latter would be a situation in which subjects

who have been excluded from enfranchisement by existing conventions (including racist conventions) governing the exclusionary definition of the universal seize the language of enfranchisement and set into motion a "performative contradiction": claiming to be covered by that universal, they thereby expose the contradictory character of previous conventional formulations of the universal.

This kind of speech appears at first to be impossible or contradictory, but it constitutes one way to expose the limits of current notions of universality, and to constitute a challenge to those existing standards to revise themselves in more expansive and inclusive ways. In this sense, being able to utter the performative contradiction is hardly a self-defeating enterprise; on the contrary, it is crucial to the continuing revision and elaboration of historical standards of universality proper to the futural movement of democracy itself. To claim that the universal has not yet been articulated is to insist that the "not yet" is proper to an understanding of the universal itself: that which remains "unrealized" by the universal constitutes it essentially. The universal begins to become articulated precisely through challenges to its existing formulation, and this challenge emerges from those who are not covered by it, who have no entitlement to occupy the place of the "who," but who nevertheless demand that the universal as such ought to be inclusive of them. The excluded, in this sense, constitutes the contingent limit of universalization. And the universal, far from being commensurate with its conventional formulation, emerges as a postulated and open-ended *ideal* that has not been adequately encoded by any given set of legal conventions.[4] If existing and accepted conventions of universality *constrain* the domain of the speakable, this constraint produces the speakable, marking a border of demarcation between the speakable and the unspeakable.

The border that produces the speakable through the exclusion of certain forms of speech becomes an operation of censorship exercised through the very postulation of the universal. Does every postulation of the universal as an existent, as a given, not codify the exclusions by which that postulation of universality proceeds? In this instance and through this strategy of relying on *established conventions of universality*, do we unwittingly stall the process of universalization within the bounds of established convention, naturalizing its exclusions, and preempting the possibility of its radicalization? The universal can be articulated only in response to a challenge from (its own) outside. What constitutes the community that might qualify as a legitimate community that might debate and agree upon this universality? If that very community is constituted through racist exclusions, how shall we trust it to deliberate on the question of racist speech?

The above definition of universality is distinct from an idealizing presupposition of consensus, one that is in some ways already there. A universality that is yet to be articulated might well defy or confound the existing conventions that govern our anticipatory imaginings. This last is something other than a pre- or postconventional idealization (Habermas) conceived as always already there, or as one already encoded in given international law (Matsuda), a position that equates present and ultimate accomplishments. It is the futural anticipation of a universality that has not yet arrived, one for which we have no ready concept, one whose articulations will only follow, if they do, from a contestation of universality at its already imagined borders.

The notion of "consensus" presupposed by either of the first two views proves to be a prelapsarian contention, one which short-circuits the necessarily difficult task of forging a universal consensus from various locations of culture, to borrow Homi Bhabha's title and phrase, and the difficult practice of translation among the various languages in which universality makes its varied and contending appearances.[5] The task of cultural translation is one that is necessitated precisely by the performative contradiction that takes place when one with no authorization to speak within and as the universal nevertheless lays claims to the terms. Or, perhaps more appropriately phrased, the extension of universality through the act of translation takes place when one who is excluded from the universal, and yet belongs to it nevertheless, speaks from a split situation of being at once authorized and deauthorized (so much for delineating a neatly spatialized "site of enunciation"). That translation is not the simple entry of the deauthorized into the authorized, whereby the former term simply alters its status and the latter domain simply makes room for what it has unwittingly failed to accommodate. If the norm is itself predicated on the exclusion of the one who speaks, one whose speech calls into question the foundation of the universal itself, then translation on such occasions is to be something more and different than an assimilation to an existing norm. The kind of translation that exposes the alterity within the norm (an alterity without which the norm would not assume its borders and "know" its limits) exposes the failure of the norm to effect the universal reach for which it stands, exposes what we might underscore as the promising ambivalence of the norm.

The failure of the norm is exposed by the performative contradiction enacted by one who speaks in its name even as the name is not yet said to designate the one who nevertheless insinuates his or her way into the name enough to speak "in" it all the same. Such double-speaking is precisely the temporalized map of universality's future, the task of a postlapsarian translation the future of which remains unpredictable. The contemporary scene of cultural translation emerges with the presupposition that the utterance does not have the same meaning everywhere, indeed that the utterance has become a scene of conflict (to such a degree, in fact, that we seek to prosecute the utterance in order, finally, to "fix" its meaning and quell the conflicts to which it gives rise). The translation that takes place at this scene of conflict is one in which the meaning intended is no more determinative of a "final" reading than the one that is received, and no final adjudication of conflicting positions can emerge. Without this final judgment, an interpretive dilemma remains, and it is that interpretive dilemma that is the dynamic mark of an emerging democratic practice.

Thus it makes little sense to imagine the scene of culture as one that one might enter to find bits and pieces of evidence that show an abiding faith in an already established notion of universality. If one were to enter various domains of culture in order to find examples of world citizens, one would invariably cull from those various examples the selfsame lesson, the selfsame universal bearing. But is the relation between culture and the universal appropriately construed as that between an example and the moral dictum it is said to support? In such cases, the examples are subordinate to the universal, and they all indicate the universal in the same way. The futural articulation of the universal, however, can happen only if we find ways to effect cultural translations between those various cultural examples in order to see which versions of the universal are proposed, on what exclusions they are based, and how the entry of the excluded into the domain of the universal requires a radical transformation in our thinking of universality. When competing claims to the universal are made, it seems imperative not to presume that the cultural moments at issue exemplify a ready-made universal. The claim is part of the ongoing cultural articulation of universality, and the complex process of learning how to read that claim is not something any of us can do outside of the difficult process of cultural translation. This translation will not be an easy one in which we reduce every cultural instance to a presupposed universality, nor will it be the enumeration of radical particularisms between which no communication is possible.

The risks will be that translation will become an imposition of a universal claim on a culture that resists it, or that those who defend the universal will domesticate the challenge posed by alterity by invoking that very cultural claim as an example of its own nascent universality, one which confirms that such a universality is already achieved. What kind of cultural imposition is it to claim that a Kantian may be found in every culture? For whereas there may be something like a world reference in moral thinking or even a recourse to a version of universality, it would sidestep the specific cultural work to be done to claim that we have in Kant everything we might want to know about how moral reasoning works in various cultural contexts.

Importantly, then, the task that cultural difference sets for us is the articulation of universality through a difficult labor of translation. That labor seeks to transform the very terms that are made to stand for one another, and the movement of that unanticipated transformation establishes the universal as that which is yet to be achieved and which, in order to resist domestication, may never be fully or finally achievable.

Richard Falk
Revisioning Cosmopolitanism

MARTHA NUSSBAUM'S POWERFULLY ARGUED
and artfully constructed cosmopolitan initiative challenges the political imagination at a historically relevant
moment to transcend the blinkered realism of modern
patriotic conceptions of loyal citizen and sovereign state
that associate political duty and identity with territorial
boundaries. One recent nationalist response to criticism
about its narrowness of outlook is for adherents to the
patriotic side of the debate to extend their ethical consciousness to the larger reality of humanity by incorporating "human rights" into their ethical convictions.
Cosmopolitan adherents welcome this outreach beyond
the exclusivities of nationalism and statism but find
such an expression of solidarity with humanity as a
whole too peripheral to achieve an appropriate reloca-
tion of ethical orientation.

Despite sharing Nussbaum's essential vision, I am
disturbed by its implicit encouragement of a polarized
either/or view of the tension between national and cosmopolitan consciousness. In so doing, it engenders a

discussion that inevitably overlooks the originality of our political circumstances in the late twentieth century—an originality that makes both poles problematic.

The patriotic pole reflects the reality of the sovereign state as the organizing basis of international society. Priority is naturally given here to national consciousness as the orienting basis for education, socialization, aspiration, and loyalty. This kind of orientation presupposes a degree of autonomy and primacy for the sovereign, territorial state that no longer exists and, if recoverable, will require deep structural changes at national, regional, and global levels of social, political, and economic organization. At present, the autonomy and primacy of the state is being seriously and cumulatively compromised, if not challenged, and even superseded, by various types of regionalization and globalization, especially by complex forms of economic, ideographic, and electronic integration. The impact of such trends on the capacity of states to promote material standards of the most disadvantaged portions of national and foreign populations is particularly severe. As such, the option and possibility of the *humane state* is disappearing in the haze of global consumerism and the heavy-metal rhythms of popular culture. In this atmosphere of diminished autonomy, the domestic choices between conservative and liberal are losing their traditional significance, as political parties of varying ideological legacy are under virtually irresistible pressure to adapt to the discipline of the global market. This logic of conformity is also diminishing, in many respects, the more fundamental distinctions between authoritarian and democratic political systems, and even between adherents of Marxist-Leninist principles and those deriving from the market-oriented constitutionalism of the West.

This dynamic if stultifying convergence is partly a consequence of the new ascendancy of foreign economic policy in constructing the domestic programs of government, particularly inducing left-liberal and social-democratic political parties and leaders to abandon their traditional humanistic goals to join with their conservative "adversaries" to reduce taxes, roll back wages and welfare, promote privatization and the free flow of capital, and generally adapt to the pressures exerted by regional and global market forces. Because this pattern can be traced globally in many diverse settings, it seems correct to treat it as a structural and defining attribute of the current phase of international history. Its specific consequence is to preclude for the indefinite future the reestablishment of the humane state.

In my view, the ethical viability of patriotism depends on sufficient political space at the level of the state to enable the emergence and maintenance of the humane state and to make such a project feasible and meaningful at the level of citizen participation. The "Swedish model" is paradigmatic of this possibility, and its demise expresses the current era of globalization. If Sweden can no longer be Sweden because of the pressures being exerted by global capital to reduce taxes, hold wages, downsize welfare, and avoid any kind of judgmental posture in foreign policy of the sort previously associated with Swedish neutrality, then to continue to rely on a nationalist orientation in the quest for political fulfillment seems increasingly to be a courtship with self-delusion. Sweden has temporarily avoided self-delusion by its forced march into the European community—a step taken democratically, but at the cost of Sweden's right to be Sweden!

Economic unevenness means the humane state can still achieve impressive results in several Asian countries afflicted in the past with massive poverty. Malaysia, South Korea, Taiwan, China, and others have manifested this potentiality, although the considerable material achievements of each is yet to be matched by upholding the full range of human rights of its citizens. Raising material and social standards, while seeking regional stability and global equity, makes possible the emergence of new types of humane states, despite the eclipse of the phenomenon in its northern birthplace.

My contention is that for social-democratic and left-liberal world views the humane state is being displaced by a reality that is as yet insufficiently understood, which I provocatively label "the neurotic state." In essence, globalizing pressures induce governing leaders and aspiring political parties to embrace policies that contradict their own defining ethical identity: structural factors overwhelm value preferences. Bill Clinton's presidency illustrates and confirms this trend: the scandalous neglect of homelessness and poverty combined with the ardent, unconditional embrace of the North American Free Trade Agreement (NAFTA) and the General Agreement on Tariffs and Trade (GATT) as indispensable ingredients of American well-being. Of course, if Clinton's deviation from the moral expectations of liberal Democrats were an isolated phenomenon, it would be natural to explain this embrace of the neoliberal consensus as episodic or a reflection of the peculiar turn to the right in America, but what has occurred, with variations here and there, is truly a worldwide pattern, characteristic of every left-of-center government and political party in recent years. Mitterand's socialism veered similarly midway through his final presidential term, and Tony Blair's spectacularly successful redirection of the British Labour Party is a further case in point. Such a trend suggests that traditional patriotism, basing itself on the humanistic potentialities of the national community, is now a self-contradictory posture, making its line of anticosmopolitan argumentation unconvincing to the extent that it evades the challenges of globalization, including its own submission.

But surprisingly, the cosmopolitan orientation is not much more satisfactory on these matters. The Stoic-Kantian vectors of a cosmopolitan orientation assume an ethical context for globalist affirmations that is increasingly difficult to reconcile with the actuality of contemporary globalism. True, the cosmopolitan outlook is explicitly ethical and humanistic on a global scale, but it is not sufficiently distinguished from or even aware of globalist tendencies that are integrating experience across boundaries at a rapid rate. To project a visionary cosmopolitanism as an alternative to nationalist patriotism without addressing the subversive challenge of the market-driven globalism currently being promoted by transnational corporations and banks, as well as currency dealers and casino capitalists, is to risk indulging a contemporary form of fuzzy innocence. A credible cosmopolitanism has to be combined with a critique of the ethically deficient globalism embodied in neoliberal modes of thought and the globalism that is being enacted in a manner that minimizes the ethical and visionary content of conceiving of the world as a whole.

The structures of regional and global economic governance are taking root in a variety of settings, including the European Community, NAFTA, the economic summits of the Group of Seven, the nascent World Trade Organization, IMF/World Bank. The rationale for such frameworks is almost entirely market-oriented and economistic, emphasizing contributions to trade and investment, efficiencies of production and distribution, and procedures for reducing the relevance of sovereign states, especially their intrusion of people-oriented protectionist, social, and local factors that help the weak withstand the strong. Such a globalism has almost no affinity with the Stoic moral imagination projected so vividly by Martha Nussbaum; it is a perspective of the whole that is totally oblivious to the ethical imperatives of human solidarity. It is typified by the McDonald's arch, the homogeneity of international hotel chains and worldwide auto rental agencies, CNN's presentation of political reality, and the universal presence on T-shirt logos of the animated characters created by Walt Disney Studios. Without a more careful clarification, there is a danger of conflating the emergent regionalisms and globalism that are reconstituting the world with those exalted cosmopolitan expectations and hopes that invoke the prospect of a genuine "species consciousness" and draw upon classical images of an ethically unified human community.

TWO SORTS OF PROPOSALS SEEM RESPONSIVE TO THESE considerations. First, inquiry into education, ethical ambition, and political loyalty needs to be recast to avoid a polarizing choice between patriotism and cosmopolitanism. Such recasting envisions continuous political conversation and an ethos of inclusiveness rather than an emphasis on the exclusive correctness of either pole. The shape of world order can no longer be reduced to the relations between parts (conceived as states) and the whole (conceived as the world). Transnational and grassroots participants and processes, including voluntary associations of citizens, now engage in many varieties of action covering the spectrum from the extreme local to the global commons and beyond, and are often animated by an ethical consciousness that gives contemporary reality to the cosmopolitan outlook. Because this consciousness is created out of this fabric of transnational social forces, it could perhaps be identified as neocosmopolitanism. Its characteristic embodiment can be illustrated by either the Greenpeace efforts to prevent Shell Oil from sinking an oil rig with toxic properties in the North Sea, or by the worldwide campaign in 1995, especially intense in the South Pacific, to protest the resumption of French nuclear weapons tests. It is a type of globalization-from-below that is people- (and nature-) oriented and contrasts with globalization-from-above that is capital-driven and ethically neutral.

The second modality of recasting focuses on the framework of political participation that follows from this type of ethical transnationalism. Patriotism in the traditional sense assumes the potential moral agency of the sovereign state. If that agency is being eroded, then the grounds of loyalty are undermined, at least from the perspective of human betterment and meaningful community.

To take better account of globalizing tendencies (from above and below) we need to disengage the practice of democracy from its traditional state/society nexus, and to acknowledge and promote what David Held has usefully identified as "cosmopolitan democracy." The global conferences organized under the auspices of the United Nations on such topics as women, development, population, and the environment are vivid expressions of this innovative democratic ethos, involving more dynamic forms of interaction between people and structures of authority, with both the participation and locale situated in a manner that contrasts with traditional domains of democratic practice centering on electoral rituals and representative institutions. These conferences do not themselves manifest cosmopolitan governance, but are rather early experiments in global or cosmopolitan democracy. They suggest new styles of and potentialities for participation, accountability, and representation, but do not yet embody these styles in distinct authority structures that normalize practice and expectations.

The extensions of cosmopolitan democracy suggest a possible reconciliation of nationalism and cosmopolitanism. If global economic governance structures are reoriented to express a kind of equilibrium between market-oriented (globalization-from-above) and people-oriented (globalization-from-below), then it is possible that political space will be recreated to enable the reemergence of the humane state. It is worth recalling that the earlier manifestations of the humane state emerged as a consequence of an equilibrium within territorial states that balanced the logic of the market against the social logic of the labor movement, and that the capitalism of the early nineteenth century rested on predatory behavior of unregulated market behavior that produced such social ills as child labor, unsafe working conditions, and job insecurity, while regulated capitalism later introduced workplace standards, labor unions and strikes, as well as minimum wages and social security. At present, the neurotic state is trapped between the compromises produced by social regulation of marketplace behavior and the new dynamics of essentially unregulated economic globalism. These competing forces commonly produce divergences between promises and performance of a depth and consistency that transcend the typical behavior of politicians who promise too much or who tilt their performance to satisfy an array of special interests.

Citizens are now being challenged to reconfigure the outmoded dichotomy between undifferentiated patriotism and cosmopolitanism. If this challenge is met, then the vitality of traditional patriotism can be restored, but only on the basis of extending ideas and practices of participation and accountability to transnational sites of struggle. If ethical, and with it political, revitalization is thwarted by the sheer weight of economic globalism—a kind of negative cosmopolitanism—then citizens with humanistic agendas will find little comfort in either patriotic or cosmopolitan poles of the current debate. If, by contrast, the debate is recast, then patriotism and cosmopolitanism will be able to share a common commitment to refashioning conditions for the humane state, the humane region, and, depending on the success of transnational social forces, a decent, inclusive globalism.

Nathan Glazer

Limits of Loyalty

In 1994, President Clinton announced a change in our Cuban refugee policy. Cuban refugees had for thirty years been favored, and this favoritism has been criticized as both racist—when compared with treatment of Haitian refugees, for example—and politically biased, rejecting a universal and uniform standard in favor of refugees from Communist regimes. I wonder what one can make of this change of policy in light of the standard Martha Nussbaum would have replace the common understanding, which she considerately calls "patriotism" rather than "nationalism" or "chauvinism." In this prevailing standard, the highest political loyalty is to one's country. Certainly President Clinton had the interests of the United States in mind when he made this change. Were he truly a world citizen, what would this imply about refugee policies?

I use the term *political* as in "highest political loyalty," because I acknowledge that no loyalty should be higher than loyalty to one's religion or to basic human values. But as I read Martha Nussbaum, she is not only arguing against the principle My country, right or wrong. We would all, patriots and cosmopolitans, allow that there comes a time when our country's policies must be resisted (which policies, and how resisted, would of course raise further difficult questions). She clearly is after something more than this, as one sees when she presents as questionable the sentiment, "I am an Indian first, a citizen of the world second." This suggests that something like world citizenship should replace American citizenship.

I have practical objections to this, but also, I believe, principled objections. The practical objections are immediately raised by the example of the Cuban refugees, and they are numerous. Is our government to treat the fleeing Cubans the way it would, for example, American citizens, permanent residents, immigrants who have gone through the proper procedures, or refugees who have established their bona fides as escaping from persecution? If so, then what distinctions should it make among those who wish to settle in this country? Should it make none? Should it defer in the matter of immigration policy to some world body, a committee of the United Nations, perhaps? Is this what the status of world citizenship suggests or requires?

Any immigrant or refugee policy presupposes a state, with rules that differentiate among those who are allowed entry, in what status and with what rights. This presupposition does not mean that those outside the boundaries of the state are without human claims, indeed rights—rights that have been in large measure specified and defined by international protocols. So, we will join in feeding the Rwandan refugees, perhaps join in protecting them, but we will not, for example, give them rights to enter the United States. All these commitments to others' claims and rights involve costs, in money and lives, and these costs are not assessed against the world, but against the citizens and soldiers of a specific country, the only entity that can lay taxes and require soldiers to obey orders. It is perhaps this reality that also gives the citizens of a state the ethical right to make distinctions. It is hard to see, practically, how to move beyond a situation in which the primary power to grant and sustain rights rests with constituted sovereign states. I suspect that one reason why cosmopolitanism could make sense to the philosophers Martha Nussbaum has studied is that they were citizens of a "cosmopolis"—a near-universal state and civilization—whose uniformity in rights and obligations was mirrored by a uniformity in city layouts and architecture. (Even their cosmopolitanism, however, may have been stretched when they thought about barbarians and Parthians.) But our situation is radically different.

The issue is more than practical. It is a problem of how far bonds of obligation and loyalty can stretch. In some respects, as I've indicated, they can encompass all men and women. Do we not sense, though, whatever the inadequacy of our principled ethical arguments, that we owe more to our family members than to others? The greater closeness of bonds to one's country and countrymen need not mean denigration and disrespect for others. Certainly there can be no argument with the position that we should know more about other countries, that we learn more about ourselves in studying them, that knowing more may help in dealing with international problems, that there are moral obligations to the rest of the world.

But there is a meaning and significance to boundaries, in personal life and in political life, as well as a practical utility. Most people around the world seem to want their governments to be smaller and less distant than they are now, rather than give power to larger, more cosmopolitan power centers. Consider how in this century empires have been reduced to a host of squabbling countries—the Ottoman, the Austro-Hungarian, the Russian, with perhaps the Chinese next. In our own country, federalism shows surprising life, and many want to devolve more and more functions that have been taken on by the national government to the states, and beyond that, to cities, counties, even individual schools.

Cosmopolitan values have made considerable headway, certainly in the more developed part of the world, where, for example, European loyalty slowly gains on national loyalty. But in the developing world, we should realize, resistance to cosmopolitan values is strong. The advocacy of cosmopolitan values is often viewed suspiciously as an arrogant insistence by formerly colonial powers that their values, Western values, be adopted. Even Singapore, that model of successful modernization and Westernization in the economic sphere, is no candidate for cosmopolitanism in the political arena, or when it comes to culture.

Cosmopolitan political loyalty is a difficult concept to make real and to free from its inevitable connection with the Western cultural tradition. That, after all, is where it comes from. We see fragments of cosmopolitanism emerging as various international treaties and commitments begin to limit the behavior of states for the good of the entire world, as in agreements on the environment, on the treatment of refugees, on the rights of women, but all are contested vigorously, all depend on the acceptance of sovereign states to make them effective, and even the oldest international agreements, on the use of violence to settle international disputes and on the kind of weapons that may be used in warfare, are regularly transgressed.

Ideally, one can envisage on one hand an extension of such understandings, and their greater effectiveness in time, together on the other hand with a devolution of many powers and functions to lower levels of government, not as remote as the national government or the even more remote international agencies, and closer to people, which is what it seems most people want.

Daniel Bell once wrote that our national states seem too small for some functions, too large for others. In an age of powerful multinational corporations, aspiring multinational institutions, and a spreading demand for the recognition of distinctive identities that we call "multiculturalism," that certainly seems to be the case. But the process of change must be mediated by the only institutions that have legitimacy and power, national states. There is no other way to implement those aspects of cosmopolitanism that appeal to us. Regarding many other aspects (for example, political loyalty, culture) we may properly remain skeptical whether a cosmopolitan world would be better than the one we have.

Amy Gutmann

Democratic Citizenship

"PROPONENTS OF NATIONALISM IN POLITICS
and in education," Martha Nussbaum writes, "frequently make a weak concession to cosmopolitanism." They say that "although nations should in general base education and political deliberation on shared national values, a commitment to basic human rights should be part of any national education system. . . ." Nussbaum identifies my defense of democratic education with this position, which she says is "a fair comment on practical reality" but not a sufficient moral ideal. The nationalism she describes is not compatible with democratic education. It neither fairly reflects practical reality nor expresses an attractive moral ideal. Practical reality is far worse, and a moral ideal of democratic education demands far more.

Most nations do not teach, let alone practice, anything close to basic human rights, which include rights to freedom of speech and religion, due process and equal protection under the law, education and economic security, and equal representation in a genuinely democratic politics. As this incomplete list indicates, basic human rights are so extensive that teaching them cannot be fairly characterized as a *weak* concession to anything. If most nations effectively taught basic human rights, practical reality would be immeasurably better than our present reality.

The same cannot be said for basing education and political deliberation on shared national values, whatever those values happen to be. This nationalistic view is abhorrent. It's strange, to say the least, that Nussbaum associates a defense of democratic humanism and democratic education with such a view. How does she manage to do so? She identifies as nationalistic the idea that a public education system should teach children the skills and virtues of a democratic citizenship that dedicates itself to furthering liberty and justice for all. She then translates this idea into the advocacy of teaching national values, whatever they happen to be. But such advocacy would clearly be incompatible with a commitment to the teaching of democratic humanist values.

What are democratic humanist values? They subsume basic human rights but also go beyond them in morally important ways. All children—regardless of ethnicity, religion, gender, race, or class—should be educated to deliberate together as free and equal citizens in a democracy that is dedicated to furthering social justice for all individuals, not just members of their own society. Are democratic humanist values "national values," as Nussbaum suggests by way of criticism? Only in the innocuous sense that they recommend themselves to be taught within the United States and every other society as part of common public education. But in this sense, Nussbaum's cosmopolitan values are also national values, and can be misleadingly tarred by the same nationalistic brush. Putting labels aside, I suspect that Nussbaum and I agree children should be taught to respect the dignity of all individuals. They should also be empowered as democratic citizens. Both are necessary (and compatible) conditions for a just democracy. The constitution of just democracies, in turn, is necessary to achieve justice in the world.

This is also the cosmopolitan view of Kant, but it is a cosmopolitanism that roundly rejects Nussbaum's claim that our "allegiance is to the worldwide community of human beings." Yes, we have duties to respect the rights of individual human beings the world over, and schools the world over should teach children (not indoctrinate them) to appreciate these duties. But it does not follow that we are "citizens of the world" or that our "fundamental allegiance" is to the community of human beings in the entire world. This cosmopolitan position might be attractive were our only alternative to give our primary allegiance to the United States of America or to some other politically sovereign community. But we have another alternative, which Nussbaum neglects (and does not recognize as the position defended by democratic humanism): to reject the idea that our primary allegiance is to any actual community, and to recognize the moral importance of being empowered as free and equal citizens of a genuinely democratic polity.

Why not empower individuals as citizens of the entire world? We can truly be citizens of the world only if there is a world polity. Given what we now know, a world polity could only exist in tyrannical form. Nonetheless, we need to be citizens of some polity to be free and equal, and we need therefore to be educated to those (particular as well as universal) skills, understandings, and values that secure full participation and equal standing in our own polity. Being empowered as a free and equal citizen of some democratic polity should be an opportunity open to all individuals. Democratic citizenship is an essential demand of justice in the world as we know it, and individuals the world over recognize it as such.

Does this emphasis on democratic citizenship imply that students in our society should therefore "learn that they are, above all, citizens of the United States" (another repugnant position that Nussbaum seems to attribute to me)? Far from being a sufficient standard for a democratic humanist education, such teaching is clearly antithetical to it. It is one thing to say that publicly subsidized schooling should teach students the rights and responsibilities of democratic citizenship (something Nussbaum never clearly recognizes) and quite another to say it should teach them that they are "above all, citizens of the United States." Our primary moral allegiance is to no community, whether it be of human beings in our world today or our society today. Our primary moral allegiance is to justice—to doing what is right. Doing what is right cannot be reduced to loyalty to, or identification with, any existing group of human beings. Morality extends even beyond the current generation, for example, requiring that we consider the well-being of future generations.

Suppose that we leave behind both the view that Nussbaum articulates—that the community of human beings in the entire world commands our primary allegiance—and the view she mistakenly attributes to democratic humanists, that "national boundaries are morally salient." We are left with an important distinction, which Nussbaum collapses in her criticism, between taking national boundaries as morally salient and recognizing them as politically salient, and likely to be so for the foreseeable future. A philosophy of democratic education rejects the idea that national boundaries are morally salient. If they are politically salient, however, then public education ought to cultivate in all students the skills and virtues of democratic citizenship, including the capacity to deliberate about the demands of justice for all individuals, not only for present-day citizens of the United States. Deliberating about the demands of justice is a central virtue of democratic citizenship, because it is primarily (not exclusively) through our empowerment as democratic citizens that we can further the cause of justice around the world.

What is Nussbaum's cosmopolitan alternative? To teach students that their primary allegiance is to the community of human beings in the entire world. Where is there any such community? There are human beings throughout the world and they are entitled to be treated as equals, according to principles of right and justice. If this is what Nussbaum means by community, she is agreeing with what democratic humanists say. If she means to refer to a community with claims that take precedence over these rights, a community that requires its members to respect those claims "above all" because they are "above all" citizens of the world, then she is recommending a vision that we should reject. It is another parochial form of nationalism, this time on a global scale. Its parochialism may be concealed by the fact that Nussbaum supplies little or no content to the world community's values. She talks about how we should understand more about other people's "histories, problems, and comparative successes," but this does not address the question of what the world community's moral values are. Understanding other people's situations, although undoubtedly important, is not the main aim of moral education. Respecting every person's claims of justice is. What are those claims? Nussbaum does not say. Were she to give cosmopolitanism content, it would look a lot like democratic humanism. By giving content to these potentially compatible ideals, we can find the common ground that we need to move beyond more abstract slogans.

Democratic humanism supports an education that encourages citizens to deliberate about justice as part of their political culture—justice for their fellow citizens as well as their fellow human beings, who are citizens of other societies. What is the cosmopolitan alternative? Publicly subsidized schools could teach students that it is their duty as individuals, regardless of their role as citizens, to further justice. We do have duties of justice quite apart from our role as citizens. But this lesson is incomplete, both morally and politically speaking, and its incompleteness helps explain why democratic citizenship is morally important. Our obligations as democratic citizens go beyond our duties as politically unorganized individuals, because our capacity to act effectively to further justice increases when we are empowered as citizens, and so therefore does our responsibility to act to further justice. Democratic citizens have institutional means at their disposal that solitary individuals, or citizens of the world only, do not. Some of those institutional means are international in scope (the United Nations being the most prominent example), but even those tend to depend on the cooperation of sovereign societies for effective action.

By teaching students to deliberate about justice as democratic citizens, not only as individuals, schools can encourage citizens to support effective institutional ways of moving toward a better society and a better world. Schools should also teach students that there are demands of morality and justice that do not depend on democratic citizenship for their realization—for example, the demands of family and friendship. But to teach either lesson with intellectual integrity, schools must move beyond the morally misguided and politically dangerous idea of asking us to choose between being, above all, citizens of our own society or, above all, citizens of the world. We are, above all, none of the above.

Gertrude Himmelfarb

The Illusions
of Cosmopolitanism

I WAS INOCULATED AGAINST COSMOPOLITAN-
ism at an early age. In a freshman history course shortly
after the outbreak of the Second World War, the professor explained that what we were witnessing was the last
gasp of nationalism—nationalism in its death throes.
Nationalism had been a nineteenth-century phenomenon, the romantic by-product of the nation-state in its
prime. It had barely survived the First World War, and
the Second would surely bring it to an end, ushering in
a cosmopolitan order committed to the universalist ideals of the Enlightenment. The professor, a scholar of
much distinction, spoke with great authority, for he had
personal as well as professional knowledge of his subject. A recent German émigré, he had intimate, tragic
experience of that anachronism known as nationalism.

Yet even then, as a sixteen-year-old, I knew something was wrong with his scenario. I recalled, from earlier lectures in the course, that the Enlightenment itself
had given birth to an aggressive nationalism. And as a

Jew I was painfully conscious of the virulent nationalism that had recently transformed an eminently enlightened, civilized country into a barbarous, murderous one.

Neither did my flirtation with Trotskyism, in my early college years, allay my skepticism about the imminent triumph of cosmopolitanism. I was prepared to believe in much of the Marxist doctrine—the class struggle, the inevitability of revolution, the triumph of the proletariat—but not in the withering away of the state. The example of the Soviet Union, reinforced by a reading of Michels and Pareto, hardly inspired confidence in that particular tenet.

If I had any lingering cosmopolitan fantasies, they were dispelled after the war, when I attended an Independent Labour Party convention in London. The convention unanimously and enthusiastically approved a resolution in favor of a United Europe. Visas, passports, and all the other stigmata of citizenship would be abolished, and Englishmen and Europeans would be united in a common brotherhood. (This was when "brotherhood" was still a permissible term.) Immediately thereafter the convention was called upon to approve another resolution—in favor of an independent Scotland. As I remember it, that motion too was unanimously accepted.

MARTHA NUSSBAUM'S ESSAY BRINGS BACK THOSE youthful memories. At a time when the European Union is confronting a multitude of problems and "Euroskepticism" is rife in all the countries belonging to that Union, when the British Commonwealth barely exists, when bloody nationalist wars have been raging in what used to be Yugoslavia and what remains of the Soviet Union, when nationalism allied with religious fundamentalism is a perpetual threat in the Mideast, and when multiculturalism in the United States challenges the very idea of *E Pluribus Unum*,

Nussbaum boldly calls upon us to reassert the ancient ideal of cosmopolitanism. Our "allegiance," she says, should be to "the worldwide community of human beings." This ideal, rather than national identity, is "more adequate to our situation in the contemporary world."

Cosmopolitanism, Nussbaum assures us, does not involve the creation of a "world state." But in the following sentences (and repeatedly thereafter), she speaks of "*the* world citizen" and "world citizenship," terms that have little meaning except in the context of a state. This is not a quibble, for it goes to the heart of her essay, her effort to ground a universal morality in a universal—and stateless—community. If nationality, as she says, is "morally irrelevant" to the cosmopolitan ideal, so is the polity that defines the nation, and so is the idea of citizenship. And so too is all of history. And not only modern history, whose fundamental categories are nationality and statehood, but even the ancient history that is her special forte.

Nussbaum quotes the Stoics at some length as proponents of the idea of a universal "moral community" and "world citizenship." But she quotes Aristotle not at all. Yet Aristotle's dictum, "Man is by nature a political animal," has proved to be far more prescient than the Stoic doctrine. Aristotle's polis, to be sure, is not the modern state. But it is a polity. And not a world polity but a specific, historic polity, a government of laws and institutions by means of which—and only by means of which, Aristotle believed— man can consciously, rationally try to establish a just regime and pursue the good life.

Nussbaum speaks of the "substantive universal values of justice and right," the "world community of justice and reason," the "moral community made up by the humanity of all human beings," the "common aims, aspirations, and values" of humanity. But where can we find those substantive, universal, common values? And what are they, specifically, concretely, existentially? To answer those questions is to enter the world of reality—which is the world of nations, countries, peoples, and polities.

Nussbaum seems to be on the verge of entering that world when she asks us to consider "how variously they [the common aims, aspirations, and values of humanity] are instantiated in the many cultures and many histories." The Stoics, she tells us, insisted that an essential task of education is the "vivid imagining of the different." But she herself does not engage in the imagining of the different. If she had, she might discover that her cosmopolitan values—"justice and right," "justice and reason," "reason and the love of humanity"—are not "variously" instantiated in the many cultures and histories that make up the world. What are instantiated are quite different values, which have little in common with her own.

At the risk of lowering the tone of discourse, we might translate these exalted concepts into mundane terms to find out whether they are in fact shared by all of humanity. "Justice" might be rendered as the rule of law; or "right" as the civil rights of minorities; "reason" as the exercise of rational discourse; or "love of humanity" as the humane treatment of human beings. Not even the most ardent cosmopolitan would claim that these are the values of "humanity as a whole." On the contrary. They are not only violated in practice by a good part of humanity; they are not accepted in principle—as values—by all of humanity. They are, in fact, predominantly, perhaps even uniquely, Western values. And it is nations founded on Western principles and traditions that have tried to give them existential reality by incorporating them into their governments, laws, and institutions.

Nussbaum's catalogue of cosmopolitan values strikingly omits two that she herself must hold dear: democracy and liberty. Perhaps it is because these are even more "culture-bound," as the invidious phrase has it, than the abstract concepts of right or reason—more distinctive of Western culture than of any other. They are also more "polity-bound," one might say—more dependent on national and political institutions and, again, of Western nations and governments than of any other.

As for more specific principles and policies that Nussbaum presumably cherishes—the social programs associated with a welfare state, or public education, or religious liberty and tolerance, or the prohibition of racial and sexual discrimination—these depend not on a nebulous cosmopolitan order but on a vigorous administrative and legal order deriving its authority from the state. The first requirement of a welfare state is a state. So too the first requirement of international cooperation, which Nussbaum regards as essential for economic development, environmental protection, and "quality-of-life issues," is the existence of states capable of undertaking and enforcing international agreements. "International" has "national" as its necessary and primary ingredient.

There are other omissions here—no mention, for example, of Islamic fundamentalism, which might evoke disagreeable images of female subjugation and abuse, religious intolerance and persecution, despotic governments and caste systems, child labor and illiteracy, and other unsavory practices that are hardly consonant with the vision of a universal "moral community."

Cosmopolitanism obscures all such unwelcome facts—obscures, indeed, the reality of the world in which a good many human beings actually reside. It is utopian, not only in its unrealistic assumption of a commonality of "aims, aspirations, and values," but also in its unwarranted optimism. One might object that the Western-style, capitalist nation-state has its own deficiencies and evils. And so it does. But they are deficiencies and evils that are at least partly remediable within the framework of a democratic polity and a secure legal system. And at their worst, they pall in contrast to the deficiencies and evils of non-Western, noncapitalist countries.

ABOVE ALL, WHAT COSMOPOLITANISM OBSCURES, EVEN denies, are the givens of life: parents, ancestors, family, race, religion, heritage, history, culture, tradition, community—and nationality. These are not "accidental" attributes of the individual. They are essential attributes. We do not come into the world as free-floating, autonomous individuals. We come into it complete with all the particular, defining characteristics that go into a fully formed human being, a being with an identity. Identity is neither an accident nor a matter or choice. It is given, not willed. We may, in the course of our lives, reject or alter one or another of these givens, perhaps for good reason. But we do so at some cost to the self. The "protean self," which aspires to create an identity de novo, is an individual without identity, just as the person who repudiates his nationality is a person without a nation.

To pledge one's "fundamental allegiance" to cosmopolitanism is to try to transcend not only nationality but all the actualities, particularities, and realities of life that constitute one's natural identity. Cosmopolitanism has a nice, high-minded ring to it, but it is an illusion, and, like all illusions, perilous.

Michael W. McConnell
Don't Neglect the Little Platoons

WE DO NOT SUFFER TODAY FROM AN EXCESS OF
patriotism. It is true that young Americans know remarkably little about the cultures, histories, religions,
and aspirations of other nations. But this is not because
they are preoccupied with their own. Few young Americans know much, or care much, about the cultures, histories, religions, and aspirations even of their own nation. Our problem is a loss of confidence in any vision
of the good, and a lack of passion for anything beyond
material gratification.

How can publicly accountable schools educate in
such an intellectual climate? Every affirmation of principle is simply an attempt to "impose values" on someone
else. The teaching of any perspective (whether cosmopolitan or patriotic or something else) is deemed refuted by the mere existence of another perspective. Cosmopolitans and patriots alike are silenced by the sneers
of the village skeptic and the sensitivities of the dis-
senter.

Martha Nussbaum's call for a self-consciously "cosmopolitan" moral education is therefore welcome: at least she recognizes the need to provide a coherent moral education of some sort. But in presenting cosmopolitanism in *opposition* to "patriotism" or "national pride"—in proposing to teach children that their "fundamental allegiance" is as "citizens of a world of human beings" rather than as citizens of the United States, indeed that citizenship in the United States is "morally irrelevant"—Nussbaum's cosmopolitanism may turn out to be more destructive than constructive. It is more likely to undermine coherent moral education, which in the real world is rooted in particular moral communities with distinctive identities, by substituting a form of moral education that is too bloodless to capture the moral imagination.

An alternative view, going back at least to Edmund Burke, perhaps to Aristotle, holds that patriotism and cosmopolitanism are not at odds. Human affections begin close to home; wider circles of affection grow out of, and are dependent upon, the closer and more natural ties. Aristotle envisioned society as a hierarchy of attachments—family, household, village, and finally the polis itself—and was skeptical of the ability of any community larger than the polis to serve as a locus of fellowship or of citizenship in the strong sense. Burke put it this way: "To be attached to the subdivision, to love the little platoon we belong to in society, is the first principle (the germ as it were) of public affections. It is the first link in the series by which we proceed toward a love to our country and to mankind."

The key to moral education is to fuse the sentiments (especially love) to a teaching of the good. We begin to do good because we love our preceptors (especially our parents); we want to please them and we want to be like them. We continue to do good because that is the kind of person we have grown up to be. Later we learn that our parents (and neighbors, and church, and nation) have flaws and moral blemishes, but our affection teaches us tolerance and forgiveness.

None of this is head knowledge. It involves relationships, time, example, ceremony, play, rebuke, and most of all, love. It is, in short, not the work of the world at large. Moral education of necessity begins with those close enough to engage in these loving relationships: with parents and family, expanding to neighbors, churches, synagogues, and local schools—communities that are familiar and that are able to provide a unifying focus to the moral life. Through the study of history it extends to the nation, and ultimately to worthy objects in the world. But its source of strength lies in the affections, which must begin close to home and radiate outward.

Effective cosmopolitanism is therefore a by-product of moral education in a great tradition. It comes when students recognize in other cultures a parallel to that which they love in their own and tolerate the flaws in other cultures just as they tolerate flaws in their own.

A student who cares not a whit for his own culture's accomplishments is unlikely to find much value in the accomplishments of others. A student who has no religion is unlikely to respect the religious commitments of others. One who knows no heroes in his own land will feel nothing but contempt for the naivete of those who honor heroes elsewhere. Before a child can learn to value others he needs to learn to value.

Burke himself was a great illustration of the connection between national pride and regard for others. Devoted husband and father and great defender of the tradition of the English constitution, Burke was the very embodiment of the patriot. Yet he devoted the bulk of his career—at enormous political cost to himself—to defending Irish Catholics, the masses of India, and American colonists from exploitation and oppression at the hands of his compatriots. And like Martin Luther King Jr. in our time, Burke did this not by appealing to universal principles *against* the patriotic impulses of his own nation, but by appeal to the national tradition itself. Burke, like King, invoked universal principles of natural right, but not as a perspective alien to the national character. Both sought to educate their countrymen in the idea that the principles of their national identity were betrayed by violations of human right. They thus appealed to the better part of our nature, and avoided the role of the outsider, critic, or scold.

Teach children instead to be "citizens of the world," and in all likelihood they will become neither patriots nor cosmopolitans, but lovers of abstraction and ideology, intolerant of the flaw-ridden individuals and cultures that actually exist throughout the world.

Humanity at large—what we share with other humans as rational beings—is too abstract to be a strong focus for the affections. Since "the world" has never been the locus of citizenship, a child who is taught to be a "citizen of the world" is taught to be a citizen of an abstraction. Abstract cosmopolitanism may well succeed in introducing skepticism and cynicism regarding the loyalties that now exist, but it is unlikely to create a substitute moral community.

Nussbaum appears to recognize this difficulty when she comments that the writings of Marcus Aurelius create a feeling of "boundless loneliness, as if the removal of the props of habit and local boundaries had left life bereft of any warmth and security." Cosmopolitanism, she admits, "offers no such refuge; it offers only reason and the love of humanity, which may seem at times less colorful than other sources of belonging." But she does not recognize that this is inherent in the project of directing the affections toward objects so distant that they have no reality in the life of a child. Love cannot be directed toward "humanity"; it can be directed only toward real people, with whom one can have a real relationship.

Moral education in a cosmopolitan vein is thus likely to turn out not only too weak to be useful in its own right, but destructive of the moral communities that have managed to persist in the face of Western materialism and cynicism. In his *Tract Relative to the Popery Laws*, Burke wrote:

> To commiserate the distresses of all men suffering innocently, perhaps meritoriously, is generous, and very agreeable to the better part of our nature,—a disposition that ought by all means to be cherished. But to transfer humanity from its natural basis, our legitimate and home-bred connections,—to lose all feeling for those who have grown up by our sides, in our eyes, the benefit of whose cares and labors we have partaken from our birth, and meretriciously to hunt abroad after foreign affections, is such a disarrangement of the whole system of our duties, that I do not know whether benevolence so displaced is not almost the same thing as destroyed, or what effect bigotry could have produced that is more fatal to society.

If cosmopolitanism is seen as opposing localized attachments, it will most likely prove destructive of these ends. To call these closer ties of nation, community, or religion "morally irrelevant" (Nussbaum's words) is to undermine the very basis of our natural sociality. Such a teaching is more likely to be received as a justification for selfish individualism than as an inspiration to generous cosmopolitanism. We will not love those distant from us more by loving those close to us less.

An abstract cosmopolitanism, moreover, is not just "less colorful" (hence less likely to form the basis for an effective moral education). It also has the danger of breeding contempt for our actual fellow citizens, who likely will remain mired in their parochialism, as well as for good people elsewhere, similarly mired. No actual culture is cosmopolitan, in the sense that Nussbaum uses the term. Each is parochial in its own way. The moralistic cosmopolitan, therefore, is not one who everywhere feels comfortable but who everywhere feels superior.

We get a faint hint of this in Nussbaum's claim that cosmopolitanism "offers only reason and the love of humanity." This might be taken to suggest—wrongly—that the various noncosmopolitan moral systems that flourish on the earth reject "reason" and the "love of humanity." Nussbaum cannot possibly mean that; if she did, it would be a sign of a parochialism far more profound than that she denounces in her essay. Surely a part of any serious cosmopolitanism is the recognition that (at least some) other cultures and belief systems are striving, in their own way, after reason and goodness, even if their method and conclusions differ from the cosmopolitan's own.

Nussbaum's advice is particularly perverse for the nation most likely to adopt it: the United States. Whatever might be true of the cultures of other lands, American culture already affirms universal norms of natural justice, rather than the pride and honor of any particular race or nation. Even America's propensity for self-criticism and recognition of past and present moral failings stands in the great tradition of the Puritan jeremiad. What better models of cosmopolitan virtue can we find for our children than those we celebrate in our public holidays, whether Washington or Lincoln or King? The particular pride of being an American is based on self-evident truths of universal application and in the appropriation of parts of the cultures of peoples, our ancestors, from every corner of the globe. What a mistake it would be to cast this aside!

Another particular problem with Nussbaum's position is her dismissal of one of the most powerful resources available for combatting selfishness and narrow national self-interest: religion. Religion, like cosmopolitanism, cuts across national boundaries and enjoins us to care for the alien and the stranger. Yet Nussbaum treats religion as nothing more than one of our "special affections and identifications," in the same category with "ethnic or gender-based" ties, all of which should be subordinated to cosmopolitan allegiance. She does not know her allies. There is something peculiar about invoking the ancient teachings of the Stoics and the Cynics in support of ideas that are taught every week in Sunday school.

In the cultural crisis of our time, solutions are not to be found in abstractions like cosmopolitanism, but in renewal of our various intact moral communities. I predict that those in the next generation who have the greatest knowledge of and respect for other cultures, as well as commitment to their own, will not be the products of an explicitly cosmopolitan education, but of home schooling, of religious schooling, of schooling in culturally and morally self-confident communities. They will be the students who learn to love the good and to recognize and respect visions of the good in others. Let us stop making life so difficult for them.

Robert Pinsky

Eros against Esperanto

WHEN I SAW THE TITLE OF MARTHA NUSS-
baum's essay, I was excited because I admire the author
and because the two words yoked as her topic raise essential matters. My disappointment with what she has
written is balanced by respect for what she begins to
open.

The patriotic and the cosmopolitan: these are not
mere ideas, they are feelings, indeed they are forms of
love, with all the terror that word should imply. In many
ways they are opposed forms of love, suggesting a pri-
mal conflict: if patriotism suggests the pull of a parental
home, cosmopolitanism suggests the pull of the marketplace, the downtown plaza. (I am told that the oldest
meaning of *kosmos* is "village.") Nussbaum's essay expresses fear toward the eros of patriotism, but fails to
imagine a counterbalancing eros of the cosmopolitan.
For the cosmopolitan she substitutes the universal, a
more abstract, less historical conception. This error is
like confusing an historical tongue such as English with
a construct like Esperanto.

The cosmopolitan is local, and it is historical.

The conflict between home and marketplace, hearth and agora, known and unknown, may have some special poignancies for the United States. Genres we invented, like the Western and the gangster movie, appeal in an almost formulaic way to rapid change across generations that migrate outward and away from what was home. The forms of jazz and rock embody the eclectic, syncretic interchange of colliding origins. Never united by being a single folk culture, still less united under any ancient aristocracy, we have at our best improvised an ever-shifting culture palpably in motion—a culture, I would say, that clarifies the fact that all cultures are motion. Insofar as the chauvinist refers to any human group or making as a static purity, the chauvinist elevates an illusion.

At our best, we contain multitudes—multitudes not merely of souls, but of *patrias*: the paradox of a culturally polyglot, ever more syncretic homeland—a cosmopolitan *patria*. At our worst, we protect some thin idea of our homeland with the fierce, despairing paranoia of the profoundly rootless. This is a basic, ancient conflict. The paradoxical ideal of reconciling the pull of home and of market, the patriotic and the cosmopolitan, is an underlying energy of the *Odyssey*, epic of seagoing pirate-traders who believed both in venturing out on Poseidon's ocean—the hero learns the ways of many different peoples, say the first lines—to seek profit and gloss, and in coming home to Ithaca. Martha Nussbaum raises the pertinent question of what this conflict should mean in the present.

But alas, her essay is provincial; it stays within the language and conceptions of a narrow place. In her first paragraph, she defines the cosmopolitan as "the person whose allegiance is to the worldwide community of human beings." Based on her "experience working on international quality-of-life issues in an institute for development economics connected with the United Nations," she defines knowledge of other countries as "their histories, problems, and comparative successes." She suggests that the young study these problems and comparative successes and that they "be taught that they are, above all, citizens of a world of human beings with the citizens of other countries." She sees India, of all places—India, container of many universes of mores, arts, sights, smells, languages, dances, poetries, sexualities, colors, gods, horrors and ecstasies—as one of a series of concentric circles, with its problems of hunger and pollution related to "larger problems of global hunger and global ecology." On behalf of the largest, outer circle of the universal, she reassures us that "we need not give up our special affections and identifications, whether ethnic or gender-based or religious."

My criticism of these arid formulations is not merely stylistic, though their sterility points to their weakness. Nussbaum is a gifted writer, but the sentences she lapses into here present a view of the world that would be true only if people were not driven by emotions. These formulas about concentric circles and global community would be valid only if cultures and nations were as static and lucid as so many bar graphs and pie charts. We do share only one world and set of resources, but we cannot deal with such facts by declaring, as by UN resolution, that we are a community.

I have the impression that some of the fiercest nationalisms and ethnocentrisms of the world are fueled in part by resentment toward people like ourselves: happily situated members of large, powerful nations, prosperous and mobile individuals, able to serve on UN commissions, who participate in symposia, who plan the fates of other peoples while flying around the world and staying in splendid hotels. Shouldn't this reality be the starting place of such discussions—or at least included in them? Shouldn't we recognize that our own view, too, is local?

In short, Nussbaum falls into the formulation of one peculiar province, the village of the liberal managerial class. I do not mean to be excessively scornful toward this conceptual village, a realm where the folk arts are United Nations institute reports and curriculum reform committees and enlightened social administration: like other villages it has within it valuable customs and individuals. But its inhabitants characteristically fail, as Nussbaum so spectacularly fails, to achieve precisely what she calls for—understanding others, comprehending the eros of what is different from home through the eros of home. To put it very simply, I think that her essay fails to respect the nature of patriotism and similar forms of love.

Nussbaum quotes Marcus Aurelius: "Accustom yourself not to be inattentive to what another person says, and as far as possible enter into that person's mind. . . . Generally, one must first learn many things before one can judge another's action with understanding." The weight of these quotations, for me, is to warn us how extreme an act of imagination paying attention to the other must be, in order to succeed even a little. Embedded in what Marcus Aurelius says is a caution against the arrogance that would correct *your* provinciality with the cosmopolitanism of *my* terms. The Muslim or Marxist or Rastafarian might draw Nussbaum's same Stoic diagram of concentric circles, but the labels would build toward a different, less cozy idea of the universal.

Lecturing us about "jingoism" is but another form of provinciality. Attachments to homeland or group are forms of love. I have spoken of the terror that word entails. When patriotism takes horrible forms, the ruling force is not some logical error, but the distortions of passion. Until Nussbaum follows the advice of Marcus Aurelius and understands "as far possible" the erotic component of the assassination of the World Cup player whose blunder caused his country's defeat, she is only talking to her fellow villagers— which is to say she is only talking.

Yet her project is noble, for she is asking, implicitly, whether there is in fact an eros of the marketplace equal to the eros of *patria*. Lévi-Strauss raises this question more darkly in *Tristes To-*

piques by positing the idea that the marketplace removes differences, reduces distinctions, and effaces delicate structures. Does the place of interchange destroy cultures by homogenization, or does it foster culture by a kind of chemical reaction? Unwittingly, the aridity of Nussbaum's Universal—a realm where even "copulation" becomes a matter of principle—suggests the bleaker likelihood.

Nussbaum presents her ideas as a set of suggestions for educating the young. The utopianism of her formulations is so bloodless that I would sooner stick with what is: with the varying, feeble mixture of vague "basics" and half-hearted, constantly changing special area "studies" that the young presently get from—well, from the marketplace. By omission, Nussbaum makes an inadvertent argument for studying works of imagination.

As to the threat of our own patriotism, the erotic spirit of the cosmopolitan does exist, to balance it or temper it. Maybe it is the powerful seduction of the marketplace that creates a defensive, viciously paternal protectiveness in nationalism, ethnocentrism, and other "patriotic" ideologies. Yet certain other instances of regionalism, ethnic pride, *afición*, even outright patriotism, can seem cosmopolitan to me—maybe because I grew up when many immigrant families routinely flew the flag on national holidays, with no meaning of self-righteousness or reactionary politics. Even the very flag itself: This summer, in the hilly farm country around Saratoga, New York, near the Erie Canal, I saw a line of laundry hung between a telephone pole and the window of a tidy-looking apartment over a country grocery store—the classic procession of clean clothes in the sun, and pinned at the end nearest the window an American flag. The informality and idiosyncrasy of this gesture—practical, intuitive, inventive, and resourceful in the way of Odysseus—seemed in the spirit of the cosmopolitan to me, as patriotic gestures go, because it put the flag into the world of daily life, flapping above the market downstairs.

In order to discuss *afición*, it may be necessary to risk the accusation of sentimentality. For me the spirit that reconciles the homeward and outward forms of eros was represented, before I had any of these terms, by the Brooklyn Dodgers: the team of Jackie Robinson and of Roy Campanella, the Italian-African-American catcher, the team adored by a borough that was in certain ways to New York what New York was to the country: historic and raw, vulgar and urbane, many-tongued and idiosyncratic, a borough of Hispanic blacks and Swedish carpenters, provincial enough to have its own newspaper yet worldly beyond measure, commercial and outward, a marketplace if there ever was one.

This ideal is not universal but historical. It is not provincial, yet it is local. It is not chauvinistic but generous and egalitarian. It is an act of the imagination, and it corresponds to reality.

One might object that actual Brooklyn was far uglier than I supposed in my *afición* for the Dodgers. One might add that not only was I a child, but except for trips to Ebbets Field I was not even *in* Brooklyn—I was in a small town on the Jersey Shore. Nevertheless, that Brooklyn of the Dodgers is a cultural reality shared by many, and I am proud to be among them. Call it patriotism.

The Brooklyn of the Dodgers has changed, it is gone, as gone as the Dodgers are gone. But it was always gone, everything is going, going, gone, because culture is change, it is movement: that is the knowledge of the cosmopolitan, and only the embrace of this form of change has the erotic appeal to counterbalance patriotism. And there is a present, successor Brooklyn that presumably contains some excellence that we can predict no more than the aged Henry James could predict, in the streets of the East Side that overwhelmed and depressed him, the already living soul of George Gershwin. It is the appeal of unknown coasts and islands that counterbalance the love of our Ithaca—which is itself an unknown island, terrible and alluring.

Hilary Putnam

Must We Choose between Patriotism and Universal Reason?

As I READ IT, MARTHA NUSSBAUM'S STIMU-lating essay is concerned to defend two ideas: first, that patriotism[1] has a strong tendency to produce national chauvinism and racism (or at least indifference to other nations, cultures, and peoples) and should therefore be marginalized, if not completely abandoned. We should think of ourselves first and foremost not as American, or French, or Black, or Chicano, or Jewish but as "citizens of the world." The second idea is that we need not (and should not) look to our various national and ethnic traditions for moral guidance at all; instead we "citizens of the world" should look to something she calls "universal reason."

The first idea bears a striking similarity to a thesis I have often heard advanced (I do not know whether Martha Nussbaum herself subscribes to it, however): that all the various realizations of the human religious impulse—all of the religious traditions, and the many different communities of faith within each that try to keep their traditions alive while interpreting them in an ever-changing world—should be discouraged, indeed scrapped if possible, because religion, it is said, always leads to fundamentalism and intolerance (some secular thinkers simply identify religion with fundamentalism and intolerance), and these, as we know, manifest themselves in the marginalization of other traditions, as well as, in the worst case, all the horrors of religious persecution and "holy war." (To see how great the similarity is to Martha Nussbaum's thesis, imagine someone saying, "All the various realizations of the human patriotic impulse—the national traditions, and the many communities within each national tradition that try to keep the national traditions alive while interpreting them in an ever-changing world—should be discouraged, indeed scrapped if possible, because patriotism always leads to chauvinism and intolerance, and these, as we know, manifest themselves in the marginalization of other peoples, as well as, in the worst case, all the horrors of ethnic cleansing and wars of extermination or subjugation." Is this not close to Nussbaum's argument for cosmopolitanism?)

What this argument does in either of its forms—the militant atheist form or the militant cosmopolitan form—is confuse a *pretext* for human aggression and cruelty with human aggression and cruelty themselves. "Remove this or that pretext, and we will have a less cruel and aggressive world," we are, in effect, being told in each case. But there is not the slightest reason to believe this. The Union of Soviet Socialist Republics, while it existed, was supposed to be completely "internationalist" (i.e., cosmopolitan). Indeed, in principle, it was hoped that one day *all* countries would be "Soviet Socialist Republics." It was also, of course, militantly atheist. Yet current Russian estimates of the victims of Stalin's crimes run upwards of 50 million persons! "But it is unfair to bring in the Soviet Union," it will be objected; "the Soviet Union wasn't *really* socialist, wasn't really internationalist, wasn't really antireligious, because communism was itself a religion," etc. But the fact remains that Stalin found plenty of supporters, even without the pretexts of religion[2] and nationalism.[3] "But," it might be argued, "the Soviet Union wasn't a democracy." Presumably, the point of saying that would be that when one *does* have a democracy, one doesn't get aggression unless nationalist or religious fervor have been whipped up. But *that* isn't true, either.[4]

Still, it could be said, if patriotism is even a major pretext for marginalizing other peoples (when we do not actually make violent war upon them), why *shouldn't* we get rid of it? What good is it? And this brings me to Martha Nussbaum's second idea, the idea of universal reason.

Let me say, first of all, that it is strange that this idea comes from her pen. Indeed, it is so out of keeping with what she has written about the moral life in her many wonderful books that I am puzzled as to whether she can really mean what she wrote; perhaps she was overreacting to Rorty.

It seems to me that a besetting problem with philosophical discussions for and against the idea of universal reason is that moral philosophers tend to be partisans either of "the good" (by which I mean to gesture vaguely at the whole area of "the good life") or of "the right" (by which I mean to gesture equally vaguely at the whole area of "justice"). Even when they acknowledge that neither sphere—neither the sphere of the good life, nor the sphere of justice (or "duty," or "obligation," etc.)—can actually be *reduced* to the other, they often tend to regard the less favored sphere as subjective (as Kant, in the *Second Critique*, regarded the sphere of the good,[5] and as utilitarians regard any talk of right or justice that is not reduced to calculations of happiness or utility). But—and here I feel sure that Martha Nussbaum and I are in agreement—both spheres are essential to our moral lives, and neither is simply subjective (which is not to say that we are not often subjective about the good and the right).

The reason this is relevant is that although maxims[6] concerning

justice are often universal, in the sense of being found wherever reflection on the moral life takes place, maxims that make it the rule
not to murder, steal, commit rape, commit adultery, or lie, and en-
join us to cooperate with our fellow humans, be loyal to friends,
and so on, are examples, although of course what is a permissible
exception to these rules is something on which there is no universal agreement—there is no such thing as a universal conception of
"the good life."

Why is this? First, of course, because there isn't just one form of
life that is "good." The life of a genuinely spiritual religious community, the life of a group of inspired bohemian artists, the life of a
dedicated group of community organizers, the life of a creative
group of computer programmers, and many other lives can all be
good in utterly incompatible ways (of course, they can also be terrible). And second, because good lives do not just spring from rational insights, in the way in which the proof that the area of a circle
is π times the square of the radius sprang independently to the
minds of ancient Greek and ancient Chinese mathematicians. Like
forms of painting or music or literature, ways of life require centuries of experimentation and innovation to develop. But in the absence of such concrete ways of life, forms of what Hegel called
Sittlichkeit, the universal maxims of justice are virtually empty, just
as in the absence of critical reason, inherited forms of Sittlichkeit
degenerate into blind tenacity and blind allegiance to authority.
Tradition without reason[7] is blind; reason without tradition is
empty.

Martha Nussbaum speaks of a pair of "cosmopolitan" philosophers who demonstrated their reliance on what she calls universal
reason—by copulating in public! But her own example tells against
her thesis, for the sense or senselessness of such an act depends on
its relation to the surrounding ways of life and their value or lack of
value; one cannot simply decide that it is silly to wear clothes, or

silly to refrain from copulating in public because universal reason did not dictate the ways of life one is deliberately flouting. The philosophers of Martha Nussbaum's own example confuse the two very different ideas of a *universal ethics* (universal principles of right) and a *universal way of life*, and argue, in effect, that any Sittlichkeit that is not part of a universal ethic construed as a universal way of life is simply absurd. (To see the error, imagine what we would say to someone who argued that good music should not presuppose any prior acquaintance with a musical tradition, but only universal reason.)

It is because *this* notion of universal reason—as something independent of all traditions—is so indefensible that Martha Nussbaum's notion of cosmopolitanism has, in the end, so little appeal for me. Like most of my contemporaries, I have inherited or acquired more than one "identity": I am an American, a practicing Jew, a late-twentieth-century philosopher. But it would never occur to me to say that I am a "citizen of the world." If I were asked, for example, why discrimination is wrong, I would *not* say "because we are all citizens of the world."

To a theist, I might say "because we are all made in the image of God." To someone to whom this would seem absurd, I might quote Dickens's beautiful remark (in *A Christmas Carol*) about Scrooge coming to see other people as "fellow passengers to the grave," or I might mention Primo Levi's haunting statement that the look an official in the concentration camp gave him "was not the look a man gives a man."[8] That someone is a fellow human being, a fellow passenger to the grave, has moral weight for me; "citizen of the world" does not. And that has to do, I think, with the fact that appeals to the notion that we are made in the image of God, or to sympathy with all other human beings, while they appeal to *potentials*, which are indeed universal, also have a long history in the traditions to which I belong, traditions we inherit.

It may be that "citizen of the world" will one day have that kind of moral weight and that Martha Nussbaum will have been the prophet of a new moral vision. But it doesn't today.

My appeal to traditions, and my defense of their necessity, should not be misunderstood. As I have argued elsewhere,[9] something we have learned from the conduct of moral inquiry itself is that inherited moral beliefs can be criticized, and that discovery is the truly precious legacy of the Enlightenment. But without inherited ways of life there is nothing for criticism to operate on, just as without critical reason there is no way for us to distinguish between what should be saved (perhaps after reinterpretation) and what should be scrapped from our various traditions. We should not make the mistake Isaiah Berlin warns us against, of accepting "Voltaire's conception of enlightenment as being identical in essentials wherever it is attained"; a conception that implies that "Byron would have been happy at table with Confucius . . . and Seneca in the *salon* of Madame du Deffand." But this is just the conception of enlightenment shared by Martha Nussbaum's pair of ancient philosophers.

An example may help to make my position clear. I believe that we need to condemn the conditions that poor people everywhere daily experience as unjust, as contrary to the most elementary principles of morality, and not simply as contrary to "our" values, in the style of Richard Rorty. Indeed, traditional morality has plenty of resources for justifying such a condemnation (recall that Augustine rejected the rationalizations offered for Roman imperialism by saying that they presupposed that the Roman Empire was a moral institution, but in fact it was no such thing—"The great Empire is a great piracy"). But it is one thing to say that poverty is an injustice that people inflict on other people, and not a law of nature; it is another thing to say what can and should be done about it. This latter requires not "universal reason" in the traditional philosophical sense, which is supposed to require nothing more than armchair reflection, but the kind of critical learning from experience that John Dewey advocated (which he called "intelligence," precisely because of the connotations of "reason" in the philosophical literature). The alternative to the kind of universal reason that Martha Nussbaum's Cynics thought they had available to them is *situated intelligence.*

I am no relativist. Like Martha Nussbaum, I believe that there is such a thing as reasoning well about moral issues. But, I repeat, actual reasoning is necessarily always situated within one or another historical tradition. To be sure, members of different traditions can and do enter into discussion and debate. But (as Dewey also stressed) in such discussions we typically find ourselves forced to renegotiate our understanding of reason itself. Because reason calls for such endless renegotiation, it cannot function as a neutral source of values for "world citizens" to live by, while they view their own cultural inheritances as if they were merely the loved (to be sure) but regrettably parochial families one happens to have. We all have to live and judge from within our particular inheritances while remaining open to insights and criticisms from outside. And that is why the best kind of patriotism—loyalty to what is best in the traditions one has inherited—is indispensable. In sum, we do not have to choose between patriotism and universal reason; critical intelligence and loyalty to what is best in our traditions, including our national and ethnic traditions, are interdependent.

Elaine Scarry

The Difficulty of
Imagining Other People

THE WAY WE ACT TOWARD "OTHERS" IS
shaped by the way we imagine them.[1] Both philosophic
and literary descriptions of such imagining show the
difficulty of picturing other persons in their full weight
and solidity. This is true even when the person is a
friend or acquaintance; the problem is further magni-
fied when the person is a stranger or "foreigner." Cruelty to strangers and foreigners has prompted many
people to seek ways to prevent such actions from recur-
ring. Some solutions envision a framework of cosmopolitan largesse that relies on the population to sponta-
neously and generously "imagine" other persons, and
to do so on a day-by-day basis. Alternative solutions, in
contrast, attempt to solve the problem of human
"otherness" through constitutional design: they seek to
eliminate altogether the inherently aversive structural
position of "foreignness."

We have the obligation to commit ourselves to both
solutions. But I weight my comments to the sphere of
constitutional design, because if this solution is in place

then the spontaneous acts of individuals have a chance of producing generous outcomes. By contrast, if constitutional solutions to foreignness are not in place, then the daily practice of spontaneous largesse will have little effect, and all our conversations about otherness will be idle. It may at first appear that the constitutional alternative only protects people within the borders of a given country, but we will eventually see that ensuring a deep regard for "foreigners" outside the borders also requires constitutional design.

Are there large numbers of people who advocate the imaginative solution over the constitutional one? The answer is yes. Even many of those German intellectuals most passionately dedicated to stopping injuries to Turkish residents often ignore altogether any discussion of altering German citizenship laws and concentrate instead on practices that can be summarized under the heading of "generous imaginings." Meetings among international scholars dedicated to human rights often express an indifference to, or impatience with, national protections on rights, and rely exclusively on international formulations. And discussions about foreignness among American intellectuals—like Martha Nussbaum's defense of cosmopolitanism—display an increasingly shared animus against "nationalism," which is perceived to be an impediment to "internationalism."

But on close inspection such attempts to replace nationalism by internationalism often turn out to entail a rejection of constitutionalism in favor of unanchored good will that can be summarized under the heading of generous imaginings. It is therefore important to come face to face with the limits on imagining other people, since in several different spheres an overly optimistic account is used to legitimate the bypassing of legal provisions and constitutional procedures. My worry about the cosmopolitan bypassing of constitutionalism is twofold. The first is the erasure of any authorizing base for the ethical principle one wants to see enforced: if twenty scholars from twenty different countries believe a certain right should be protected, they may feel, as they speak with one another, that their views rise above "mere" nationalism; but in fact their views only represent the beliefs of twenty people (a much smaller number than the population of even the smallest country), unless the populations of the various geographical areas from which they come have themselves voted to uphold the given right. Human rights are universal in content, but they are particular in their base of authorization and enforcement.

My second ground of concern, the one to which I address myself here, is the misconception of the imagination that often inspires the wish to rise above parochial constitutionalisms.

I. The Difficulty of Imagining Others: The Case of "Enemies"

The difficulty of imagining others is shown by the fact that one can be in the presence of another person who is in pain and not know that the person is in pain. The ease of remaining ignorant of another person's pain even permits one to inflict it and amplify it in the body of the other person while remaining immune oneself. Sustained and repeated instances of this are visible in political regimes that torture.

I focus on physical injury here because other forms of well-being—voting rights, access to education, the daily possibility of interesting work—are all premised on bodily inviolability. Indeed, the social contract comes into being precisely to minimize bodily injury. Locke, a physician as well as a political philosopher, repeatedly uses the word "injury" in his *Second Treatise of Government*. Though the "injury" is not specified as, or limited to, bodily injury, it takes its force from that original context. Locke uses the verb "injures" both where the object is the material reality of the body and where the object is freedom,[2] just as he speaks of invading another's body, invading another's property (the "annexed body"), or instead invading another's rights.[3] When Locke uses the idiom of "invasion" for a nonphysical object, he often immediately follows it by the word *rapine*, to restore the physical referent.

The strong relation between the social contract and the diminution of injury is visible in social contracts that long antedate the Lockean contract. In the eleventh and twelfth centuries, many of the five hundred major European cities came into existence through explicit acts of oath taking and contract making.[4] Often called "sworn communes," "conjurationes," or "communes for peace," their very names memorialized the extraordinary verbal process by which they had come into being. In the language of these city compacts, as in the Lockean compact, we can hear the key association between self-governance and the diminution of injury. The founding of Freiburg, for example, emphasizes the guarantee of "peace and protection."[5] The Flemish charter of Aire promises, "Let each help the other like a brother."[6] And one oath for mutual assistance from the Bologna region states that the members should "maintain and defend each other against all men, within the commune and outside it."[7]

The town's commitment to protecting its members from outside aggression by no means implied that outsiders were themselves subjected to aggressive treatment. Outsiders who entered the city could become insiders at their own discretion. Harold Berman writes that "immigrants were to be granted the same rights as citizens [the right to vote, to bear arms, to a jury trial] after residence for a year and a day."[8] The relatively swift transformation from immigrant to citizen suggests that bearing the status of "foreigner" was itself seen to be an injurious condition and hence one that it was the obligation of the commune to remove.

Bodily injury is, then, what necessitates the social contract in both theory and practice, in both the Lockean contract and the earlier city contracts. The contract comes into being to put constraints on the act. The ease of inflicting injury (as well as the omnipresence of the impulse to injure) shows the difficulty of knowing other persons. There exists a *circular relation* between the infliction of pain and the problem of otherness. *The difficulty of imagining others is both the cause of, and the problem displayed by, the action of injuring.* The action of injuring occurs precisely because we have trouble believing in the reality of other persons. At the same time, the injury itself makes visible the fact that we cannot see the reality of other persons. It displays our perceptual disability. For if other persons stood clearly visible to us, the infliction of that injury would be impossible.

II. The Difficulty of Imagining Others: The Case of Friends

If we take as our starting point the action of injuring, we have taken the imagination at the moment when its failures, its limitations, already stand fully exposed. Let us turn instead to the "best case" picture of imagining. How fully we are able to imagine other persons can best be measured by moving away from the category of "enemy" to the category of "friend." (It is unlikely that a foreign population can ever achieve the fullness in one's imagination that a single personal friend achieves, but let us assume for the moment that such a thing would be possible.) How capacious is the imagination at its most capacious? When we speak in everyday conversation about the imagination, we often attribute to it powers greater than ordinary sensation. But Sartre's study of the imagination powerfully underscores its limits. He asks us to perform the concrete experiment of comparing an imagined object with a perceptual one—that is, of actually stopping, closing our eyes, concentrating on the imagined face of a friend or a familiar room, then opening our eyes and comparing its attributes to whatever greets us when we return to the sensory world. We find at once that the imagined object lacks the vitality and vivacity of the perceived. Even if the object we select to imagine in this experiment is the face of a beloved friend, one we know in intricate detail (as Sartre knew in detail the faces of Annie and Pierre), it will be, by comparison with an actually present face, "thin," "dry," "two-dimensional," and "inert."[9]

This description of imagining a friend illuminates the problems that await us when we rely on the imagination as a guarantor of political generosity. Transport the problems of trying to imagine a single friend to the imaginative labor of knowing the other—not an intimate friend, not any single person at all, but instead five, or ten, or one hundred, or one hundred thousand; or x, the number of Turks residing in Germany; or y, the number of illegal aliens living in the United States; or z, the estimated number of Iraqi soldiers and citizens killed in our bombing raids; or 70 million, the scale of population that stands to suffer should the United States fire a nuclear missile (a conservative estimate). Philosophic discussions of the other typically contemplate the other in the singular.[10]

What we do not do well in the singular we do even less well in the plural. The human capacity to injure other people has always been much greater than its ability to imagine other people. Or perhaps we should say, *the human capacity to injure other people is very great precisely because our capacity to imagine other people is very small.*

It might be objected that the "best case" for the powers of the imagination should be made not by assessing the daydreaming mind but the mind as it produces images under the instruction of an author.[11] To be sure, this is the place—the place of great literature—where the ability to imagine others becomes very strong. Great novels, great poems, great plays often do incite in our imaginings the vivacity of the perceptual world. During the hours of reading Thomas Hardy's *Tess of the D'Urbervilles*, Tess comes before the mind with far more fullness, surprise, vivacity, and vividness than Sartre's two-dimensional images or our own daydreams. But while novels and poems are better able than daydreams to bring other persons to press on our minds, even here we must recognize severe limits of imaginative accomplishment.

One key limit is the number of characters. A novel or poem may have one major character. Or perhaps four. It is impossible to hold rich multitudes of imaginary characters simultaneously in the mind. Presented with the huge number of characters one finds in Dickens or in Tolstoi, one must constantly strain to keep them sorted out; and of course their numbers are still tiny when compared with the number of persons to whom we are responsible in political life.

A second constraint concerns our tolerance for imaginary features that are different from our own actual features. The latent nationalism or tribalism of great literature may make it a seductive vehicle for an exercise in self-reflection and self-identification, rather than reflection upon and identification with people different from oneself. Despite, for example, the emphasis on artistic multiculturalism in the United States, it sometimes appears that Asian-American literature is being read by Asian Americans, Afro-American literature by Afro-Americans, and Euro-American literature by Euro-Americans.

A third limit is the lack of any anchor in historical reality. More often than not, fictional others lack referents in material reality. It has often been a criticism of literature that the very imaginative labor of picturing others that we ought to expend on real persons on our city streets, or on the other side of the border, instead comes to be lavished on King Lear or on Tess. Pushkin provided a stunning portrait of how we come out of the opera, absorbed with compassion for those on stage, not seeing the cabdriver and horses who are freezing from their long wait to carry us home.[12]

I have been calling attention to the limits on solving real-world otherness through literary representation alone. There are, of course, exceptional cases. Harriet Beecher Stowe's *Uncle Tom's*

Cabin made Blacks—the weight, solidity, injurability of their personhood—imaginable to the White population in pre–Civil War United States. E. M. Forster's *Passage to India* is almost the only other novel that has had an equivalent claim made for it: the book, overnight, according to Stephen Spender, enabled the British population to begin to reimagine India's population as independent. But the Stowe and Forster examples are extremely rare, both because they required readers to imagine not just "a person" but "a people," and above all because they modified the well-being of actual persons to bring about greater freedom and hence a diminution of the status of otherness. More often we must say of literature what Auden wrote in his elegy for Yeats: "Poetry makes nothing happen: it survives / In the valley of its saying."[13]

Finally and most important, even in these exceptional cases where a novel incites in one population the ability to imagine more fully a second population, the test of that new imaginative capaciousness is not in the pleasurable feeling of cosmopolitan largesse but in the concrete willingness to change constitutions and laws: the thirteenth, fourteenth, and fifteenth amendments to the U.S. Constitution; the Independence of India Act of 1947. How can such constitutional and legal changes be made if the polity, the nation-state, comes to be regarded as an object of cosmopolitan disdain?

III. Equality of Weightlessness

When we seek equality through generous imaginings, we start with our own weight, then attempt to acquire knowledge about the weight and complexity of others. The alternative strategy is to achieve equality between self and other not by trying to make one's knowledge of others *as weighty as* one's self-knowledge, but by making one ignorant about oneself, and therefore *as weightless as* all others.

This strategy of imaginative recovery has been developed by

Bertrand Russell, and more elaborately and influentially by John Rawls. Russell argued that when reading the newspaper each day, we ought routinely to substitute the names of alternative countries to test whether our response to the event arises from a moral assessment of the action or instead from a set of prejudices about the country.[14] This ethical practice, which obligates us to detach a given action from country X and reattach it to country Y, might be called "the rotation of nouns." Rawls imagines a social contract made behind a "veil of ignorance" that prevents people from knowing any of their particular traits. The veil of ignorance fosters equality not by giving the millions of other people an imaginative weight equal to one's own—a staggering mental labor—but by the much more efficient strategy of simply erasing for a moment one's own dense array of attributes. Through it we create what Rawls describes as "the symmetry of everyone's relations to each other."[15] Constitutional arrangements, too, rely on this strategy of imagined weightlessness, since they define rights and powers that are independent of any one person's personal features.

The problem with discussions of "the other" is that they characteristically emphasize generous imaginings, and thus allow the fate of another person to be contingent on the generosity and wisdom of the imaginer. But solutions ought not to give one group the power to regulate the welfare of another group in this way. Picture, for example, a town in which third-generation light-skinned residents can vote but third-generation dark-skinned residents cannot vote. The light-skinned residents—through goodwill and large-mindedness—take into consideration, before they vote, the position of the dark-skinned residents. (This is a utopian assumption, of course, given the difficulty of imagining other people; but for the sake of argument, let us suppose they are able and willing to do it.) Thus they have acted to minimize the problem of foreignness or otherness or heterogeneity by holding in their minds a picture of those other people on the basis of which they make their political decisions.

Now contrast this with a situation in which the dark-skinned third-generation residents are citizens and vote for themselves. Light-skinned residents no longer need to act on behalf of the others. Because a constitutional provision enables each group to act on its own behalf, no group any longer occupies the legal position of the other. Even if we stipulate that in the first solution the light-skinned third-generation residents act with maximum generosity and largesse, the second solution is obviously much stronger. They would, even at best, be acting paternally, and hence operating outside the frame of social contract whose purpose, as Locke argued in his *Second Treatise of Government*, was precisely to decouple paternal power from political power.

What differentiates the first and second strategies of inclusion (let us call them Town One and Town Two) is the principle of self-representation: to endorse that principle is to reject the idea of protecting people by empowering an enfranchised group to look after them by means of generous imaginings.

To stress the importance of creating laws that eliminate the structural position of the other, I have presented the acts of imagining others and unimagining oneself as two separate alternatives. Although when each is considered in isolation the second is stronger than the first, together the two are far stronger than either alone. Town Two only fully works when supplemented with Town One's magnanimous imaginings, especially when reciprocated across mutually enfranchised groups. And the importance of Town One's commitment to the imagination is particularly clear when we consider the existence of borders. While it is possible to eliminate the legal position of the Other within a country, it is not possible to do so for people outside its borders. Here the problem of otherness, with its steady danger of injury, cannot be addressed through voting rights but might seem dependent on the largess of the imagination alone. Even this cosmopolitan practice of the imagination, however, can be constitutionally encouraged and safeguarded.

Right now, for example, the United States has a nuclear policy that permits a president, acting almost alone, to authorize the firing of nuclear weapons. How should people in the United States protect other populations from the sudden use of this monarchic weapons system? Should we hope that at the moment of firing, the president will suddenly have the imaginative powers to picture other people in their full density of concerns, picture not one caricatured leader but the men and women and young people of that country? But the U. S. Constitution was written to ensure that the fate of other populations would never be left up to the accident of whether a U. S. president (or any solitary person, or forty or fifty solitary persons that might make up a presidential council or a weapons crew) happens to be resourceful at imagining other populations. It anticipates, and attempts to diminish, the problem of otherness by building in elaborate requirements for debate and deliberation both in the Congress and among the citizens, requirements that ensure that voices speaking on behalf of the about-to-be-injured population will be heard.[16] In other words, it distributes the responsibility to imagine other people to a large portion of the population. Since the invention of atomic weapons, these constitutional safeguards have disappeared. Yet within the U. S. Constitution at this very moment are the provisions—the legal tools—to prohibit, to make impossible, mass destruction.

Alarm over the disappearance of these constitutional safeguards has been muted by many factors, among them the sense on the part of intellectuals that any site bound up with the polity—such as Congress or the Constitution—is somehow a piece of parochial nationalism, hence not something whose disappearance need worry us. Thus the very agency that would constrain our weapons is ignored in the name of high-minded internationalism. International congresses such as the United Nations have a crucial role to play *if and only if* any act of national aggression requires their authorization *in addition to* the constitutionally mandated congressional or parliamentary authorization of the home country. But the deliberative actions of the UN are instead often taken as a *substitute* for congressional action. Any cosmopolitan who believes this is an admirable outcome should read the private papers of U. S. presidents throughout the second half of the twentieth century: again and again, a president will openly acknowledge how much easier it is to secure UN authorization than Congressional authorization for an act of international aggression he has wished to initiate.

Legal provisions to distribute the rights of citizenship across a country's internal population do not guarantee that those citizens will abstain from injuring one another; so, too, legal provisions to ensure that foreigners—those outside the country's borders—will be carefully imagined before a willful infliction of injury takes place cannot necessarily guarantee that their own specifications will be followed. But such legal arrangements at least objectify an aspiration; they set the standard of action, and they provide the mechanism for holding the population to its promises.

Civil society can only exist if it is produced by the constituents of that country. The major constitutive act is the making of a constitution. The *Federalist Papers* continually asked the question: What kind of arrangement will produce a noble and generous people? Perhaps every group of constitution-makers has asked this same question. Nor is it restricted to the liberal democratic ethos. Marx, in the *Grundrisse*, contrasts the question asked by contemporary economic societies—What kind of arrangements will make the most money?—with the question asked by more ancient societies, what kind of city-state will produce the best citizens? But he concludes that our present interest in production and distribution is only a partially veiled manifestation of the ancient concern with the creation of good people. Audible in works as different as the *Federalist Papers* and the *Grundrisse* is the assumption—present everywhere in the social contract theorists—that the social contract recreates us, that it is a lever across which we act on, and continually revise, ourselves. More self-revision is needed as we continue to repair our laws and prepare for a more generous future. And that self-revision will best proceed through our constitutional structures and aspirations, and not simply through a reliance on expanding our imaginings.

The work accomplished by a structure of laws cannot be accomplished by a structure of sentiment. Constitutions are needed to uphold cosmopolitan values.

Amartya Sen

Humanity and Citizenship

IF MARTHA NUSSBAUM'S INTENTION WAS TO
provoke people, she has certainly managed to do that.
This must count as success. The failure to provoke anyone in a deeply divisive subject would be good evidence
of banality. I would like to comment on an issue about
which Nussbaum has been particularly attacked. This
concerns her endorsement of Diogenes' norm, "I am a
citizen of the world," which carries the implication that
a person's "allegiance is to the worldwide community of
human beings."

Critiques of World Citizenship

Several objections have been raised to the idea of world
citizenship. I shall consider three. First, Sissela Bok is
worried that the norm Nussbaum endorses seems to
support the conclusion—which may be taught to children—that "all claims to national or other identity" are
"morally irrelevant." Bok finds Nussbaum perilously
close to William Godwin's view that "if two persons are
drowning and one is a relative of yours, then kinship

[or, presumably, nationality—Bok's addition] should make no difference in your decision as to whom to try to rescue first." Bok argues cogently, quoting Rabindranath Tagore, whom Nussbaum had also quoted, that "there is nothing wrong with encouraging children fully to explore their most local existence in order eventually to reach beyond it."

Second, Hilary Putnam attacks the rejection of patriotism that is entailed by Nussbaum's position, and argues that "the best kind of patriotism—loyalty to what is best in the tradition(s) one has inherited—is indispensable."

Third, Gertrude Himmelfarb presents the argument, among others, that the terms *world citizen* and *world citizenship* have "little meaning except in the context of a state." Michael Walzer takes a similar view. The implication of Nussbaum's position, Himmelfarb argues, is to render irrelevant "the polity that defines the nation" and even the normal idea of "citizenship"—and even "all of history." Himmelfarb also notes the importance of "justice," "right," "reason," and "love of humanity," and claims that "not even the most ardent cosmopolitan would claim that these are the values of 'humanity as a whole.'" She argues that these are "predominantly, perhaps even uniquely, Western values."

I consider these arguments in turn.

The Role of Local Identities

Bok's critique raises several interesting questions, but I believe that her concerns are not irreconcilable with Nussbaum's ethical framework. Why should a belief that one's "fundamental allegiance" is as a citizen of the world deny all sensitivity to *other* identities? The demands of *fundamental* allegiance need not be identical to those of *exclusive* allegiance. Indeed, as Nussbaum notes, "The Stoics stress that to be a citizen of the world one does not need to give up local identifications, which can be a source of great richness in life." We all have, in this view, a sequence of identities, but outside all is "the largest one, that of humanity as a whole." She does not dispute that we may have reasons for other, more particular, concerns; for example, as a city dweller, we may have particular obligations to our "fellow city dwellers." Her proposal is to make "our task as citizens of the world" include "making all human beings *more like* our fellow city dwellers" [emphasis added]. If being a world citizen would entail that we have no loyalty at all to our fellow city dwellers, then the project of making all human beings more like these uncherished creatures would scarcely help.

The point that Nussbaum is making is not unlike one Adam Smith presented. He, too, was attracted by the Stoic idea of world citizenship. Smith explained, "Man, according to the Stoics, ought to regard himself, not as something separated and detached, but as a citizen of the world, a member of the vast commonwealth of nature."[1] The kind of issue that motivates this norm is similar to Nussbaum's. Smith puts it thus:

> If he was to lose his little finger to-morrow, he will not sleep tonight; but, provided he never saw them, he will snore with the most profound security over the ruin of a hundred millions of his brethren, and the destruction of that immense multitude seems plainly an object less interesting to him, than this paltry misfortune of his own. To prevent, therefore, this paltry misfortune to himself, would a *man of humanity* be willing to sacrifice the lives of a hundred millions of his brethren, provided he had never seen them?[2]

Smith answers the rhetorical question in the negative, thereby characterizing "a man of humanity" and proceeds then to consider the Stoic norm of regarding oneself as a citizen of the world.

Sissela Bok's concern, I would argue, should relate ultimately *not* to the diagnosis of our primary allegiance, which is compatible with additional concerns for kinship and other relations, but to the need to accept multiplicity of loyalties. In the absence of such plural concerns, problems of the kind Bok describes would arise no matter where our primary allegiance lies, since the primary allegiance would then end up being our unique allegiance. Suppose our primary allegiance relates to nationality (not to all of humanity), and it is our unique—not just primary—moral concern. Then again, to stick to Bok's example, a person may not have reason enough to save first the person who has kinship relation with him or her (vis-à-vis a person who shares a nationality but is not otherwise related to her). Problems will continue to occur even if the primary and exclusive commitment is to relations, because then, given the choice, a person would save a relation, even if that involved the sacrifice of the lives of thousands of nonrelations (to whom there is no commitment). No matter where the primary allegiance is placed, so long as plural concerns are not admitted (so that primary becomes also *exclusive*), we would end up with problematic cases of various kinds.

The importance of Nussbaum's focus on world citizenship lies in correcting a serious neglect—that of the interest of people who are not related to us through, say, kinship or community or nationality. The assertion that one's fundamental allegiance is to humanity at large brings every other person into the domain of concern, without eliminating anyone. There are indeed good grounds to regard this to be primary, if our common humanity has perspicuous moral relevance. If after acknowledging that, and after a basic acceptance of concern for all, we find grounds for giving some additional weight to the interests of those who are linked to us in some significant way (such as kinship), then that can be done through the identification of a supplementary allegiance. Since the primary allegiance applies to the interests of all in a nondiscriminating way, any additional weight—no matter how small and secondary— would make the picture asymmetric (in the direction desired by Bok). The primacy of the general allegiance to humanity does not have to be disputed for this, so long as the exclusiveness of that moral reason is avoided.

To sum up, the kind of problems that worry Sissela Bok need not arise despite the primary allegiance of world citizenship, so long as the existence of a primary allegiance does not eliminate the possibility of other allegiances. And if only one kind of allegiance is permitted, then we would run into problems of the type that worry Bok, *no matter* where that primary allegiance is placed—on humanity, nationality, locality, or kinship.

While I have been trying to show that the kind of priority Bok recommends is consistent with a general system of having primary allegiance to being a citizen of the world, that primary allegiance does not, of course, entail that we *must* accept the priorities identified by Bok. There is a serious ethical issue as to whether we have good reasons to try to save our kin and relations first, over others. And even when we agree to give that preferential treatment a place, there can be several alternative grounds for doing this. There can be instrumental arguments in favor of a relational priority (for example, it may be better for "division of labor," or informationally more economic), which need not rest on any additional weight on the interests of relations (or neighbors, fellow citizens). These further ethical issues remain, and are not closed, one way or the other, by the declaration of one's fundamental allegiance to being a citizen of the world.[3] The focus on world citizenship outlined by the Stoics, Adam Smith, and Martha Nussbaum is effective in encountering a different problem: that of not excluding any person from ethical concern. It is a momentous assertion, and it seems to me to be justifiable precisely for the reasons they have identified.

Loyalty to What Is Best in the Tradition

I turn now to Hilary Putnam's objection regarding the value of loyalty to the best things within a tradition. Once again, it is not obvious why such a value, or the consequences of such a valuation, must be rejected by what Nussbaum recommends. The inclusion of everyone in the domain of ethical concern—the main point of the world citizenship claim—need not militate against valuing elements in one's own tradition.

Here, too, the possibility of additional valuations remains open even when the basic claims of all human beings are given recognition. Indeed, Adam Smith goes on to spell out the possibility of combining different values with the basic Stoic claim about world citizenship. And we know from Nussbaum's literary and philosophical work how much importance she substantively attaches to the enriching role of traditions and culture. Nussbaum's criticism is clearly aimed at certain manifestations of patriotism. The debunking of those features, which is a separate issue, may have much to commend it, but that debunking is not entailed by the claim of primary allegiance to world citizenship. For this reason, it seems important to distinguish between Nussbaum's world citizenship claim, and the rejection of some forms of patriotism, for which arguments beyond the demands of world citizenship are to be presented.

State, Values, and the Non-Western World

Can one be a citizen of the world without there being a world state? There is a legal form of language that excludes this possibility. And yet so many "mixed" concepts—human rights, libertarian entitlements, just deserts—seem to communicate well enough without being fully tied to the legal sense. When Adam Smith quoted the Stoics to support the view of a person as a citizen of the world, it was not altogether unclear what he was communicating, even though that communication was not parasitic on the presumption of a world government. His view provided one way of seeing the prior demands of our common humanity, which can of course be supplemented by additional concerns. I do not doubt that Bentham and Marx would spurn this practice, which would appear to them as the dressing up of post-legal understandings as prelegal concepts, but Smith's and Nussbaum's contentions are not based on any very eccentric use of language.

I have no great difficulty with Himmelfarb's claim that the importance of such things as justice, right, reason, and love of humanity, are not "values of humanity as a whole" (that would be a tall claim). But I do have a problem with her belief that these are "predominantly, perhaps even uniquely, Western values." I should first say that nothing much may turn on this belief, since Nussbaum's claim is not that these ideas are already shared by all, but that all people have reason to respect them. (To see that not all people, *even in the West*, actually respect them, we need not look much beyond the history of this century.) But I would also argue that Himmelfarb's argument has internal problems, because of the factual weaknesses in her sharp distinction between Western and non-Western values.

Because I have gained so much in the past from reading Himmelfarb's careful analysis of historical literature, I can only conclude that she simply has not yet taken much interest in the not insubstantial literature on these and related matters in Sanskrit, Pali, Chinese, and Arabic. For example, one may or may not agree with Ashoka that gratuitously harming person A for whom another person B has affection is also to harm B, and that justice requires that this not be done for the sake of both A and B (as he claimed in one of his famous inscriptions in the fourth century B.C.), but it would be hard to know what he was discussing if it were presumed that nothing about justice was being discussed (in a land far away from the West). As I was reading Himmelfarb's comments, I was reminded of a Bengali poem I encountered some time ago, which can be freely translated as "After all, they are not Bengali / What can they possibly know / About the meaning of such terms as mother, father, brother and sister?"

The absence of ideas of liberty and justice in so-called Asian values has been recently presented with much force by governmental spokesmen of several Asian countries, including China and Singapore (for example, in the Vienna conference of 1993, to dispute the relevance of human rights in Asia). Confucius is vigorously invoked to justify that belief. But Confucius is not the only thinker in Asia, not even in ancient China (and it is not even clear to me that Confucius is entirely more authoritarian than Plato or St. Augustine). It is true, of course, that many—though not all—of the exponents of justice or tolerance or freedom in Asian classical literature tended to restrict the domain of concern to some people, excluding others, but that is also true of the ancient West. Aristotle's exclusion of women and slaves does not make his works on freedom and justice irrelevant to the present-day world. We have to see the origin and exposition of ideas in terms of their factored components.

The liberty that is increasingly taken in quick generalizations about the past literature of non-Western countries to justify authoritarian Asian governments seems to have its analogue in the equally rapid Western belief that thoughts about justice and democracy have flourished only in the West, with the presumption that the rest of the world would find it hard going to keep up with the West. The world is perhaps less doomed than that.

Charles Taylor

Why Democracy
Needs Patriotism

I AGREE WITH SO MUCH IN MARTHA NUSSBAUM'S well-argued and moving piece, but I would like to enter one caveat. Nussbaum sometimes seems to be proposing cosmopolitan identity as an alternative to patriotism. If so, then I think she is making a mistake. And that is because we cannot do without patriotism in the modern world.

This necessity can be seen from two angles. The most important is this: The societies we are striving to create—free, democratic, willing to some degree to share equally—require strong identification on the part of their citizens. It has always been noted in the civic humanist tradition that free societies, relying as they must on the spontaneous support of their members, need the strong sense of allegiance that Montesquieu called *vertu*. This reliance is, if anything, stronger in modern representative democracies, even though they integrate "the liberty of the moderns" with the values of political liberty. Indeed, the requirement is stronger just because they are also "liberal" societies, which cherish negative liberty and individual rights. A citizen democracy can only work if most of its members are convinced that their political society is a common venture of considerable moment and believe it to be of such vital importance that they participate in the ways they must to keep it functioning as a democracy.

Such participation requires not only a commitment to the common project, but also a special sense of bonding among the people working together. This is perhaps the point at which most contemporary democracies threaten to fall apart. A citizen democracy is highly vulnerable to the alienation that arises from deep inequalities and the sense of neglect and indifference that easily arises among abandoned minorities. That is why democratic societies cannot be too inegalitarian. But to forestall excessive inequality, they must be capable of adopting policies with redistributive effect (and to some extent also with redistributive intent). And such policies require a high degree of mutual commitment. If an outsider can be permitted to comment, the widespread opposition to extremely modest national health care proposals in the United States doesn't seem to indicate that contemporary Americans suffer from too great a mutual commitment.

In short, we need patriotism as well as cosmopolitanism because modern democratic states are extremely exigent common enterprises in self-rule. They require a great deal of their members, demanding much greater solidarity toward compatriots than toward humanity in general. We cannot make a success of these enterprises without strong common identification. And considering the alternatives to democracy in our world, it is not in the interest of humanity that we fail in these enterprises.

We can look at this from another angle. Modern states in general, not just democratic states, having broken away from the traditional hierarchical models, require a high degree of mobilization of their members. Mobilization occurs around common identities. In most cases, our choice is not whether people will respond to mobilization around a common identity—as against, say, being recruitable only for universal causes—but which of two or more possible identities will claim their allegiance. Some of these will be wider than others, some more open and hospitable to cosmopolitan solidarities. It is between these that the battle for civilized cosmopolitanism must frequently be fought, and not in an impossible (and if successful, self-defeating) attempt to set aside all such patriotic identities.

Take the example of India that Martha Nussbaum raises. The present drive towards Hindu chauvinism of the Bharatiya Janata Party comes as an alternative to the Nehru-Gandhi secular definition of Indian national identity. And what in the end can defeat this chauvinism but some reinvention of India as a secular republic with which people can identify? I shudder to think of the consequences of abandoning the issue of Indian identity altogether to the perpetrators of the Ayodhya disaster.

In sum, I am saying that we have no choice but to be cosmopolitans and patriots, which means to fight for the kind of patriotism that is open to universal solidarities against other, more closed kinds. I don't really know if I'm disagreeing with Martha Nussbaum on this or just putting her profound and moving plea in a somewhat different context. But this nuance is, I think, important.

Immanuel Wallerstein
Neither Patriotism
Nor Cosmopolitanism

THE MERITS OF PATRIOTISM AND COSMOPOLI-
tanism are not abstract, and certainly not universal. We
live in a deeply unequal world. As a result, our options
vary according to social location, and the consequences
of acting as a "world citizen" are very different depending on time and space. Had there not been *swadeshi*, India would still be a British colony. Would this
have served Kantian morality more? This Gandhi
understood, but Tagore did not.

Those who are strong—strong politically, economically, socially—have the option of aggressive hostility toward the weak (xenophobia) or magnanimous compre-
hension of "difference." In either case, they remain
privileged. Those who are weak, or at least weaker, will
only overcome disadvantage (even partially) if they insist on the principles of group equality. To do this
effectively, they may have to stimulate group consciousness—nationalism, ethnic assertiveness, etc. Mandela's
nationalism was not morally the same thing as Afrikaner

nationalism. One was the nationalism of the oppressed (Blacks oppressed by Whites) seeking to end oppression. The other started as the nationalism of the oppressed (Afrikaners oppressed by English-speakers) but developed into the nationalism of the oppressor (*apartheid*).

What is the concrete situation in the United States today? In 1945, the United States became the hegemonic power in the world-system—by far the most powerful nation economically, militarily, politically, and even culturally. Its official ideological line was threefold: America is the world's greatest country (narrow nationalism); America is the leader of the "free world" (the nationalism of the wealthy, White countries); America is the defender of the universal values of individual liberty and freedom of opportunity (justified in terms of Kantian categorical imperatives).

The United States government and moral spokesmen saw no difficulty in making all three assertions simultaneously. Most persons were unaware of the internal inconsistency of this triple stance. But others—at least certain others—saw the stance as nothing more than a justification, a legitimation of United States privilege and domination. They often found it easiest to attack the hypocrisy of American Kantianism by asserting the liturgy of national liberation.

The world has moved on. The United States is not as strong as it was. Western Europe and Japan have caught up to, even overtaken, the United States in economic terms. They are in the process of detaching themselves politically. The collapse of the USSR has further weakened the United States, insofar as it has undermined the major political hold the United States had over Western Europe and Japan.

Within the United States the voice of oppressed groups has become more stridently "ethnic," relying far less on appeals to universal values than it previously did. In response to both geopolitical decline and the more ethnocentric style of oppressed groups in the United States, the defenders of privilege have resorted to demands for an "integrating" patriotism.

But the response to a self-interested patriotism is not a self-congratulatory cosmopolitanism. The appropriate response is to support forces that will break down existing inequalities and help create a more democratic, egalitarian world. The stance of "citizen of the world" is deeply ambiguous. It can be used just as easily to sustain privilege as to undermine it. One needs a far more complex stance, constantly moving toward and away from defensive assertion of the group rights of the weak as the political arena changes the parameters of the battle.

What is needed educationally is not to learn that we are citizens of the world, but that we occupy particular niches in an unequal world, and that being disinterested and global on one hand and defending one's narrow interests on the other are not opposites but positions combined in complicated ways. Some combinations are desirable, others are not. Some are desirable here but not there, now but not then. Once we have learned this, we can begin to cope intellectually with our social reality.

Michael Walzer

Spheres of Affection

I THINK I AGREE WITH EACH OF MARTHA
Nussbaum's arguments for a "cosmopolitan education";
they are quite specific and sensible. I am less convinced
by her underlying and overriding world view—perhaps
because I am not a citizen of the world, as she would like
me to be. I am not even aware that there is a world such
that one could be a citizen of it. No one has ever offered
me citizenship, or described the naturalization process,
or enlisted me in the world's institutional structures, or
given me an account of its decision procedures (I hope
they are democratic), or provided me with a list of the
benefits and obligations of citizenship, or shown me the
world's calendar and the common celebrations and
commemorations of its citizens. I am wholly ignorant;
and although a cosmopolitan education would be a very
good thing, I don't see, from Nussbaum's account, that
it would teach me the things any world citizen would
need to know. It would, however, teach me things that
American citizens need to know: Why isn't that good
enough? Can't I be a cosmopolitan American (along

with all the other things that I am)? I have commitments beyond the borders of this or any other country, to fellow Jews, say, or to social democrats around the world, or to people in trouble in far-away countries, but these are not citizen-like commitments.

Nussbaum's image of concentric circles is more helpful than her idea of world citizenship—precisely because it suggests how odd it is to claim that my *fundamental* allegiance is, or ought to be, to the outermost circle. My allegiances, like my relationships, start at the center. Hence we need to describe the mediations through which one reaches the outer circles, acknowledging the value of, but also passing through, the others. That is not so easy to do; it requires a concrete, sympathetic, engaged (but not absolutely engaged) account of the inner circles—and then an effort not so much to draw the outermost circle in as to open the inner ones out. I would read the Plutarch line that Nussbaum quotes as an opening of this sort: "We should regard all human beings as our fellow citizens and neighbors." That is, we begin by understanding what it means to have fellow citizens and neighbors; without that understanding we are morally lost. Then we extend the sense of moral fellowship and neighborliness to new groups of people, and ultimately to all people. Nussbaum's cosmopolitan works by analogy: "regard . . . as . . ." No doubt commitments and obligations are diminished as they are extended, but the extension is still valuable, and that, I take it, is the value of a "cosmopolitan education."

I suspect that Nussbaum wants something more than this, and I am a little surprised by the confidence of her cosmopolitan convictions. She is quick to see the chauvinist possibilities of Richard Rorty's patriotism, and she worries that he makes no proposal to cope with this "obvious danger." Shouldn't her readers worry that she makes no proposal to cope with the obvious dangers of cosmopolitanism? The crimes of the twentieth century have been committed alternately, as it were, by perverted patriots and perverted cosmopolitans. If fascism represents the first of these perversions, communism, in its Leninist and Maoist versions, represents the second. Isn't this repressive communism a child of universalizing enlightenment? Doesn't it teach an antinationalist ethic, identifying our primary allegiance (the class limitation, "*workers* of the world," was thought to be temporary and instrumental) much as Nussbaum does? A particularism that excludes wider loyalties invites immoral conduct, but so does a cosmopolitanism that overrides narrower loyalties. Both are dangerous; the argument needs to be cast in different terms.

III

Martha C. Nussbaum

Reply

As a visitor walks into Yad Vashem, the Holocaust memorial in Jerusalem, she comes upon a long avenue of trees. Each of these trees bears a number, a name or names, and a place. As of December 1995, there are, I believe, 1172 such trees. Each tree honors a person (or couple or family) who risked death to save a Jew or Jews. These people were *goyim*—French or Belgian or Polish or Scandinavian or Japanese or German, and atheist or Christian or members of some other religion. They had their own local identities and nationalities and, often, religions. They had friends and, in many cases, families. Sometimes some of these loyalties supported their actions; religion was frequently among their sources of support. Sometimes these loyalties opposed their choices—local politics always opposed them. These "righteous *goyim*," however, risked the loss of all that was near and dear to them to save a stranger. They did not need to do so. Everything pointed the other way. But somehow, against all odds, their imaginations had acquired a certain capacity to recognize and respond to the human, above and beyond the claims of nation, religion, and even family.

The sight of this avenue of trees can strike the visitor with a peculiarly stark terror, made all the more searing by the peaceful leafiness of the young trees, in such contrast to the monumental architecture that surrounds them. The terror, which persists, is the terror of the question they pose: Would one, in similar circumstances, have the moral courage to risk one's life to save a human being, simply because he or she is human? More generally, would one, in similar circumstances, have the moral courage to recognize humanity and respond to its claim, even if the powers that be denied its presence? That recognition, wherever it is made, is the basic act of world citizenship.

We have so many devious ways of refusing the claim of humanity. Rousseau speaks of the imagination's tendency to engage itself sympathetically only with those who resemble us, whose possibilities we see as real possibilities for ourselves. Kings don't pity subjects because they think they never will be subjects. But this is a fragile strategem, both false and self-deceptive.[1] We are all born naked and poor; we are all subject to disease and misery of all kinds; finally, we are all condemned to death. The sight of these common miseries can, therefore, carry our hearts to humanity—if we live in a society that encourages us to make the imaginative leap into the life of the other.

We also easily suppose, Rousseau adds, that people who are not like us do not really suffer as we suffer, do not really mind their pain. These obstacles in the mind were powerfully manipulated by Nazi antisemitism, which situated Jews at a distance from other citizens, constructed their possibilities as different from those of others, and encouraged citizens to imagine them as vermin or insects, who would really not suffer the way human beings suffer. And of course they let people know that to recognize human suffering would bring heavy penalties. Despite these obstacles, the people represented by the 1,172 trees recognized the human, and made this recognition the benchmark of their conduct.

My essay in defense of cosmopolitanism argues, in essence, that we should follow them and try as hard as we can to construct societies in which that norm will be realized in as many minds and hearts as possible and promoted by legal and institutional arrangements. Whatever else we are bound by and pursue, we should recognize, at whatever personal or social cost, that each human being is human and counts as the moral equal of every other. To use the words of John Rawls, "Each person possesses an inviolability founded on justice."[2]

To count people as moral equals is to treat nationality, ethnicity, religion, class, race, and gender as "morally irrelevant"—as irrelevant to that equal standing. Of course, these factors properly enter into our deliberations in many contexts. But the accident of being born a Sri Lankan, or a Jew, or a female, or an African-American, or a poor person, is just that—an accident of birth. It is not and should not be taken to be a determinant of moral worth. Human personhood, by which I mean the possession of practical reason and other basic moral capacities, is the source of our moral worth, and this worth is equal. To recognize these facts is a powerful constraint on what one may choose and on the way in which one attempts to comport oneself as a citizen. What I am saying about education is that we should cultivate the factual and imaginative prerequisites for recognizing humanity in the stranger and the other. Rousseau is correct when he says that ignorance and distance cramp the consciousness.What I am saying about politics is that we should view the equal worth of all human beings as a regulative constraint on our political actions and aspirations.

WHAT CAN THIS MEAN, WHEN THERE IS NO WORLD state? This question seems a little odd to me, given the fact that a very long tradition in concrete political thinking, beginning with

Cicero's *De Officiis* and extending through Grotius to Kant and Adam Smith and straight on to modern international law, has appealed to Stoic norms to justify certain maxims of both domestic and international political conduct.[3] Some of these include: the renunciation of wars of aggression, constraints on the use of lies in wartime, an absolute ban on wars of extermination, and the humane treatment of prisoners and of the vanquished. In peacetime, both Cicero and Kant recognize duties of hospitality to aliens working on their soil; Kant insists on a strict denunciation of all projects of colonial conquest.[4] For the entire tradition, individuals bore duties of benevolence that were loosely defined, in most cases, but understood to be extremely important and relatively demanding. Giving one's money is a major way in which, in the absence of a world state, individuals can promote the good of those who are distant from them. To say "I cannot act as a world citizen, since there is no world state" would have been seen by this tradition as a cowardly way of avoiding thinking about how high a price one will pay to help others who are in need. For one can always find ways to help, if one thinks as a member of that virtual commonwealth, which Kant called "the kingdom of ends." To quote John Rawls again, "Purity of heart, if one could attain it, would be to see clearly and to act with grace and self-command from that point of view."[5]

In our own world, moreover, there are many practical opportunities for world citizenship that were simply not available to the Stoics, or even to Kant and his contemporaries. As Richard Falk points out, nongovernmental organizations of many kinds are mobilizing to influence government action on issues ranging from ecology to domestic violence; one may support or join such organizations. Through such groups one may pressure national governments to take action toward certain global aims. The deliberations of governments, moreover, are becoming ever more intertwined and international: the population conference in Cairo and the women's meeting in Beijing are just two examples in which governments recognized the existence of problems that cross national lines. The information revolution is rapidly multiplying the possibilities for action as a world citizen. My morning newspaper today brings information about the deaths of thousands of (mainly female) orphans in China from malnutrition.[6] The very existence of such news opens possibilities of action for the world citizen, possibilities ranging from financial support for Human Rights Watch to thinking and writing to (where it is open to individuals) more direct participation in deliberations about the welfare of children and women. One can do all these things, and the fact that there is no world state is no excuse for not doing them. Increasingly, too, we are all going to have to do some tough thinking about the luck of birth and the morality of transfers of wealth from richer to poorer nations. The fact that the nation-state is the fundamental political unit does not prevent one from discovering to what an astonishing degree the luck of being born in a particular country influences life chances. To take just a single example, life expectancy at birth ranges from 78.6 years in Hong Kong and 78.2 years in Iceland and Sweden to 39.0 years in Sierra Leone.[7] This is not just, and we had better think about it. Not just think, do.

The absence of a world state does not thwart cosmopolitan conduct, then, for those who are genuinely committed to it. But cosmopolitanism does not require, in any case, that we should give equal attention to all parts of the world. None of the major thinkers in the cosmopolitan tradition denied that we can and should give special attention to our own families and to our own ties of religious and national belonging. In obvious ways, we must do so, since the nation-state sets up the basic terms for most of our daily conduct, and since we are all born into a family of some sort. Cosmopolitans hold, moreover, that it is right to give the local an additional measure of concern. But the primary reason a cosmopolitan should have for this is not that the local is better per se, but rather that this is the only sensible way to do good. Appiah's moving account of his father's career makes this point wonderfully. Had Joe Appiah tried to do a little good for all the people of the world, he would have contributed far less to the world than he did by his intense commitment to Ghana. The same holds true of parenthood: if I tried to help all the world's children a little bit, rather than to devote an immense amount of love and care to Rachel Nussbaum, I would be no good at all as a parent (as Dickens's portrait of Mrs. Jellyby mordantly showed). But that should not mean that we believe our own country or family is really worth more than the children or families of other people—all are still equally human, of equal moral worth.

A useful analogy is one's own native language. I love the English language. And although I have some knowledge of some other languages, whatever I express of myself in the world I express in English. If I were to try to equalize my command of even five or six languages, and to do a little writing in each, I would write poorly. But this doesn't mean that I think English is intrinsically superior to other languages. I recognize that all human beings have an innate linguistic capacity, and that any person might have learned any language; which language one learns is in that sense morally irrelevant, an accident of birth that does not determine one's worth. That recognition of equal worth has practical consequences for the ways in which I react to and speak about others. Similarly, in the moral case, I may focus disproportionately on the local. But my recognition of equal humanity does supply constraints on my conduct toward others. What are these constraints? May I give my daughter an expensive college education, while children all over the world are starving and effective relief agencies exist? May Americans enjoy their currently high standard of living, when there are reasons to think the globe as a whole could not sustain that level of consumption? These are hard questions, and there will and should be much debate about the proper answers. My point is that we must ask the questions, and we must know enough and imagine enough to give sensible answers.

AS WE POSE THESE QUESTIONS, WE SHOULD VALUE HUman diversity. As Appiah says, the cosmopolitan ideal includes a positive delight in the diversity of human cultures, languages, and forms of life. This pluralism prompts cosmopolitan liberals to insist on what is called "the priority of the right to the good," that is, on giving first priority to structures—prominently including structures of equal liberty—that will protect the ability of people to choose a form of life in accordance with their own lights, whether cultural or religious or personal. The very principles of a world citizenship in this way value the diversity of persons; they value it so much that they make liberty of choice the benchmark of any just constitutional order, and refuse to compromise this principle in favor of any particular tradition or religion. McConnell and I differ deeply on the issue of public funding for religious education. We do not differ, however, about the profound importance of religion, and respect for religious difference, in a just society. Our difference concerns the right way for a liberal regime to value diversity. In my view, valuing diversity entails strong support for a shared public culture that makes the right prior to the good. I believe that this goal would be subverted by public funding of religious schools, and I therefore oppose such funding. In his view, valuing diversity entails giving parents the chance to use public funds to choose a religious education for their children; to give the public schools an advantage is not fair to those who prefer religious schools. But these are differences within a larger agreement about the importance of strong protections for religious liberty. Of course, in saying this I am doing what Putnam rightly advises, valuing what is best in U.S. constitutional traditions, as well as what is best in the traditions of India[8] and, no doubt, many other places; in general, a world citizen will always try to find the seeds of the commendable universal in the local, but he or she also will be prepared to discover that some of them are missing.

The crucial question for a world citizen is how to promote diversity without hierarchy. Liberals are committed to diversity, but also to equality: They view equality as a constraint on the forms of diversity that may reasonably be fostered. Some forms of difference have historically been inseparable from hierarchical ordering: for example, racial differences in America, gender differences almost everywhere, differences of dialect or of literary and musical taste in many parts of the world. Some forms of diversity are clearly separable from hierarchy: most religious and ethnic differences, and many cultural differences. The challenge of world citizenship, it seems to me, is to work toward a state of things in which all of the differences will be nonhierarchically understood. We have no way of knowing what some of them will look like under true equality. Were gender differences to become more like the differences among ethnic groups in America or the differences between basketball fans and lovers of jazz, what would be left of them? We simply do not yet know. But that is the ideal to which the world citizen aspires. It is, of course, much better to be in a world that has both Dennis Rodman and Wynton Marsalis than in a world that has only one or the other. Both are great, and no doubt they would be less uniquely great were they more similar. We should value diversity in that way. But we should not value that part of it that is defined in terms of dominance and subordination. (This does not mean that the world citizen cannot believe that the Bulls are better than all other teams. World citizens never deny what is self-evidently true.)[9]

World citizenship, then, places exacting demands on the imaginations of each of us. To be sure, the imagination is not enough. As Adam Smith noted, compassion for others is a fragile and inconstant device. If we left our world citizenship to the vagaries of our own daily reflections, we would act less well than if we were to institutionalize our best ideas. I agree with Elaine Scarry, therefore, that the imagination needs laws—especially constitutional arrangements—that do as much as possible to institutionalize the equal worth of persons. But these laws must take their impetus from the imagination, and they will prove unstable to the extent that people become obtuse. We must, therefore, cultivate world citizenship in our hearts and minds as well as our codes of law. I agree with Scarry, for the reasons she gave and a few others, that works of imaginative literature play a pivotal role in that cultivation.[10]

WE HAVE MANY WAYS OF AVOIDING THE CLAIM OF COMmon humanity. One way, I think, is to say that the universal is boring and could not be expected to claim our love. I am astonished that so many distinguished writers should make this suggestion, connecting the idea of world citizenship with a "black-and-white" world, a world lacking in poetry. The world of the cosmopolitan can *seem* boring—to those hooked on the romantic symbols of local belonging. But many fine things can seem boring to those not brought up to appreciate them. What my critics charge, however, is that it is *right* to find the love of humanity boring, that powerful art cannot be made about it, that it is bloodless and characterless somewhat the way fast food is characterless. It seems to me, by contrast, that it would be difficult to find a powerful work of art that is not, at some level, concerned with the claim of the common and our tragic and comic refusals of that claim.

Ancient Athenian tragedy was not about a peculiarly Greek ethnicity—though of course, it derived from indigenous literary and musical traditions and could best be understood by people steeped in those traditions. It dramatized its aspiration to recognition of humanity by situating itself in mythic times, or on the Trojan side of the Trojan War—or on a desert island, home to an outcast whose foot oozes pus, whom all good Greeks shun with a properly Greek disgust. Shakespeare's deviously fictive places ("a seacoast in Bohemia") indicate a similar desire to lure the imagination away from its most complacent moorings in the local, causing it to venture outward to some strange land, be it medieval Denmark or ancient Rome, where human beings, not without poetry and not without passion, attempt to love one another, often tragically. Even the most apparently local of literary landscapes—say, Joyce's Dublin or Walt Whitman's America—are landscapes of the imagination in which the human body and its zestful surprising irregularities have a more than local home. Consider, too, how much not-black-and-white poetry and prose concerns, in fact, the situation of the exile and outsider—Philoctetes, Hamlet, Leopold Bloom, Molly Bloom—people who, by virtue of their outsider status, can tell truths about the political community, its justice and injustice, its embracings and its failures to embrace. In engaging with such works—and indeed with any works that depict a world of human beings beyond the narrow one we know—in permitting these strangers to inhabit our minds and our hearts, we are enacting the love of humanity. This does not seem boring.

In Walter Scott's famous poem, on which I was raised, the non-patriot is a man "with soul so dead" that he never could be the subject of "minstrel raptures."[11] The poem suggests that all true poetry is patriotic in inspiration and in theme. Several of my critics would appear to be followers of Scott, and I am cast as that person whose empty humanism is destined to go to its grave "unwept, unhonored, and unsung." I suggest, instead, that large-souled and compelling art is generally concerned with the recognition of the common in the strange and the strange in the common—and that narrowly patriotic art, by contrast, is frequently little more than kitsch, idolatry. Scott's poem is kitsch. Much of Rudyard Kipling's poetry is kitsch. Most of the products of most poet laureates in office are kitsch. What tragic drama could there be if one exalts one's own people above others, refusing the moral claim of a common humanity, with its common needs, failures, fears, and refusals? What lyric poetry of any depth? Tagore's point in *The Home and the World* was that Sandip only *seemed* more interesting. As both a sexual being and a rhetorical artist, he was utterly banal.

This of course does not require us to deny that all profound human matters are differently realized in different societies, or that the full understanding of any artwork involves, therefore, engagement with history, society, and the specificities of a local way of life, as well as knowledge of a literary tradition. Nor does it require denying that even the inner world of emotion, desire, and thought is differently realized in different societies, or that any real-life human being is some concrete instantiation of some specific set of human potentialities. But that we can recognize one another across these divisions—that we can even form the project of investigating them—is also true, and fundamental. Dante was a poet of his time, and we cannot read him well without learning a great deal about his time. But if he were only a poet of his time, Pinsky would not be producing his magnificent poem translating him, nor would any of us care to read his works. In such generous engagements with a stranger, we enact a duty of the moral imagination that we all too frequently shun in real life. We never do meet a bare abstract "human being." But we meet the common in the concrete, as well as the concrete in the common.

SEVERAL OF MY CRITICS SUGGEST AN ACCOUNT OF moral development that makes a mystery out of familiar experiences of commonality. It goes like this: When a child is little, it recognizes and loves only its own particular parents; then, after a while, it comes to know and love its other relatives, then its region or local group, then its nation—and finally, if at all, we get to humanity on the outside. But we come to the larger only through the smaller, and it is the moral emotions connected with the smaller that can be expected to have the most force.

Consider an alternative account. At birth, all an infant is is a human being. Its needs are the universal needs for food and comfort and light. Infants respond, innately, to the sight of a human face. A smile from a human being elicits a reactive smile, and there is reason to think this an innate capacity of recognition. At the same time, in the first few months of life an infant is also getting close experience of one or more particular people, whom it soon learns to tell apart from others, roughly at the time that it is also learning to demarcate itself from them. These people have a culture, so all the child's interactions with them are mediated by cultural specificity; but they are also mediated by needs that are in some form common, and that form the basis for later recognition of the common.

At some point, the child understands that these givers of food and comfort are also separate people, people who can go and come at will. She is learning something about her parents' particularity, but at the same time discovering a common feature of human life: that bodies are separate from other bodies, wills from other wills. This discovery leads, it would seem, to fear and anger—experiences that are always concretely shaped, but which also display much crosscultural commonality. The extreme physical helplessness of the human infant, combined with its early cognitive maturity, give human infancy a specific life course that creates a poignant combination of deep need with the awareness of the ungovernability of the sources of need—making the ambivalence of love a likely part of all human concern. A plausible view about the origin of moral thinking is that it is, at least in part, an effort to atone for and regulate the painful ambivalence of one's love, the evil wishes one has directed toward the giver of care. In atonement for having made the overweening demand to be the center of the universe, the young child agrees to limit and regulate her demands by the needs of others. Again, this learning will be concretely shaped in each different society—but the powerful motivations of a child to overcome hatred of loved ones derive from features of a common humanity. They also take the child back to that humanity, by asking her to consider herself as one person among others, not the entire world. Although this learning is about a specific mother or father, its content carries the heart to humanity.

As the child grows older and begins to hear and tell stories, she investigates further the shape of the shared form of human life. Most children's stories do not bind the mind to the local. Good fairy tales are rarely about Cambridge, Massachusetts. They inspire wonder and curiosity by exploring the contours of things both strange and surprisingly familiar. They ask children to concern themselves with the insides of animals and trees, as well as humans of many places and times. While inhabiting a particular local world, they are already learning about a far larger world. (Children frequently have more intense moral concern for animals than for the adults around them.[12] And anyone who has traveled with a child in a place of great poverty will know that the impulse of sympathy is simple and powerful in the child, devious and imperfect in oneself.) The imaginations of children are flexible and subtle instruments of acknowledgment, carrying them to the distant in the local and the familiar in the distant. All circles develop simultaneously, in a complex and interlacing movement. But surely the outer circle is not the last to form. Long before children have any acquaintance with the idea of nation, or even of one specific religion, they know hunger and loneliness. Long before they encounter patriotism, they have probably encountered death. Long before ideology interferes, they know something of humanity.

This brings me back to the avenue of trees. These people were able to function as world citizens because they had not permitted the original awareness of common needs and vulnerabilities to be eclipsed by the local. I imagine them retaining from childhood a sense of the human face, and also of their own needy hungry humanity. I imagine them retaining a vivid determination that ill wishes would not triumph over good, that their desire to subordinate their parents to their own needs would not triumph over the claims of the separate other. Because they had not allowed themselves to become encrusted over by the demands of local ideology, they were able to respond to a human face and form. In that sense, it seems to me most just to represent them as young green trees, bearers of a certain freshness, a living human thought—the thoughts of adult children, rather than of the shriveled adults we often, all too tragically, become.

Notes

Martha C. Nussbaum, Patriotism and Cosmopolitanism

1. See Hackney's speech to the National Press Club, which was circulated to all participants in the planning meeting.

2. This is an important qualification. A short essay of mine on international issues was eventually included in the Scholar's Pamphlet issued by the project: "A National Conversation on American Pluralism and Identity: Scholar's Essays," MacArthur Foundation.

3. A recent example of this argument is in Amy Gutmann's "Multiculturalism and Democratic Education," presented at a conference on "Equality and Its Critics" held at Brown University in March 1994. My article originated as a comment on Gutmann's paper. For Gutmann's reply, see "Democratic Citizenship," this volume, pp. 66–69.

4. For some related questions about women and work, see the articles in Martha C. Nussbaum and Jonathan Glover, eds., *Women, Culture, and Development* (Oxford: Clarendon Press, 1995).

5. I am grateful to Brad Inwood for permission to use his unpublished translation of this section.

6. I exempt Hipparchia from criticism, since she was clearly trying to show him up and she did not endorse the fallacious inference seriously.

Kwame Anthony Appiah, Cosmopolitan Patriots

1. Joseph Appiah, *Antiochus Lives Again (Political Essays of Joe Appiah)*, ed. Ivor Agyeman-Duah (Kumasi, Ghana: I. Agyeman-Duah, 1992).

2. Gertrude Stein, *An American and France* (1936) in *What Are Masterpieces?* (Los Angeles: Conference Press, 1940), p. 61.

3. We *don't* all agree on where the rights come from. I favor a view in which human rights are embodied in legal arrangements within and between states, rather than one in which they somehow antecedently exist or are grounded in human nature.

4. E. W. Blyden in Howard Brotz, *Negro Social and Political Thought* (New York: Basic Books, 1966), p. 197.

5. The tendency in the anglophone world to sentimentalize the state by calling it the nation is so consistent that if I had earlier referred to the "state team" or the "state anthem," they would have seemed cold, hard, and alien.

6. The expression "imagined community" was given currency by Benedict Anderson's *Imagined Communities: Reflections on the Origin and Spread of Nationalism* (London: Verso, 1983).

7. For a discussion of Herder's views, see chapter 1 of my *In My Father's House: Africa in the Philosophy of Culture* (New York: Oxford University Press, 1992).

Sissela Bok, From Part to Whole

1. Henry Sidgwick, "Some Fundamental Ethical Controversies," *Mind*, o.s. 14, 1889, pp. 473–487.

2. Henry Sidgwick, *The Methods of Ethics* (1907) (New York: Dover Publications, 1966), p. 246.

3. Rabindranath Tagore, "A Poet's School," in *Rabindranath Tagore: Pioneer in Education. Essays and Exchanges between Rabindranath Tagore and L. K. Elmhirst* (London: John Murray, 1961), pp. 63–64.

4. Rabindranath Tagore, "Siksha-Satra," in *Rabindranath Tagore*, p. 82.

Judith Butler, Universality in Culture

1. Mari J. Matsuda, "Public Response to Racist Speech: Considering the Victim's Story," in *Words that Wound*, eds. Mari J. Matsuda, Charles R. Lawrence III, Richard Delgado, Kimberlè Williams Crenshaw (Boulder, Colo.: Westview Press, 1993), pp. 26–31.

2. The following discussion on universality is taken in revised form from a forthcoming essay, "Sovereign Performatives in the Contemporary Scene of Utterance," *Critical Inquiry*.

3. Étienne Balibar, "Racism as Universalism," in *Masses, Classes, and Ideas*, trans. James Swenson (New York: Routledge, 1994).

4. See the comparable views of ideals and idealization in Drucilla Cornell and Owen Fiss.

5. Much of this discussion is indebted to Homi Bhabha's use of Walter Benjamin's notion of "translation" for thinking about the problem of exclusion in cultural politics. See Bhabha, *The Location of Culture* (New York: Routledge, 1993).

Hilary Putnam, Must We Choose Between Patriotism and Universal Reason?

1. I include loyalties to an ethnic group (even if it is not a national group) under the term *patriotism*, because Martha Nussbaum's argument applies to these.

2. Although this is not relevant to Martha Nussbaum's paper, since I have discussed an argument against religion that parallels her argument against patriotism, let me remark that the variant of the former argument that claims that *all* passionately held convictions are really "religions" simply changes the claim that religion is responsible for human intolerance and violence to the very different claim that passionately held convictions are. My own view—like William James's in *The Will to Believe*—is that what we want is not a world without any passionately held convictions, but rather a world in which people recognize that their right to their own passionately held convictions does not give them the right to force those convictions on others.

3. It is, of course, true that Stalin *also* appealed to nationalism, but this was primarily after the Nazi invasion of the country, and not to justify his purges, but rather for the—presumably laudable!—purpose of mobilizing the Russians for self-defense. The great purges were carried out in the name of defending "socialist revolution," not nationalism.

4. The Vietnam War, in which we dropped more bombs on Vietnam—a country of 17 million people—than were dropped in all of World War II, is a case in point. We never appealed to American nationalism (nor, of course, to religion) to justify our actions, but rather to "democracy," "saving the Vietnamese from communism" (by poisoning their land and napalming their children!), etc. A very popular, but completely false, claim is that "democracies do not go to war with other democracies." In fact, the United States' interventions in Chile (against Allende) and later in Costa Rica (which almost everyone seems to have forgotten) were, in reality, acts of war against democratic regimes. Similarly, the invasion of Egypt (the Suez Canal affair) by England, France, and Israel had

nothing to do with whether Nasser's Egypt was undemocratic. Nasser was, in fact, popularly elected. What is true so far is that democracies do not go to war with *powerful* democracies. But it is just not true that, even under the conditions of democracy, aggression and imperialism require religious or "patriotic" pretexts.

5. *The Critique of Judgment*, however, seems to me to mark a radical change in Kant's thought about the good.

6. I write "maxims" to bring out that it is not a question of *exceptionless rules*.

7. I do not much like the term "universal reason," however—not because the human capacity to reason *isn't* universal—of course it is!—but because the traditional associations with the notion are aprioristic and do not fit the fallible sort of learning from experience that John Dewey stressed; it is the latter that is needed in the criticism of inherited traditions.

8. Cora Diamond called both of these passages to my attention.

9. Cf. my "Pragmatism and Moral Objectivity," collected in *Words and Life* (Cambridge, Mass.: Harvard University Press, 1994), *Pragmatism: An Open Question* (Oxford: Blackwell, 1995), and "Are Moral and Legal Values Made or Discovered?" in *Legal Theory*, vol. 1, no. 1 (March 1995) (and also my replies to two critics in the same issue).

Elaine Scarry, The Difficulty of Imagining Other People

1. This brief response to Martha Nussbaum is adapted from my long essay, "The Difficulty of Imagining Other People," which originated as a lecture for a public meeting in Frankfurt about injuries to Turkish residents in Germany. The full text appears in Germany as "Das schwierige Bild der Anderen," in *Schwierige Fremdheit Über Integration und Ausgrenzung in Einwanderungsländern*, ed. F. Balke, R. Habermas, P. Nanz, P. Sillem (Frankfurt: Fischer Verlag, 1993), pp. 229-263; and will appear in English in *Human Rights and Historical Contingency*, eds. Carla Hesse and Robert Post (Berkeley: University of California Press, forthcoming).

The essay, in its long and short forms, is dedicated to Günther Busch.

2. John Locke, *Second Treatise of Government* (Indianapolis: Hackett, 1980), p. 52.

3. Locke, *Second Treatise of Government*, pp. 115-116.

4. Harold Berman, *Law and Revolution: The Formation of the Western Legal Tradition* (Cambridge: Harvard University Press, 1983), p. 393.

5. Berman, *Law and Revolution*, p. 375.

6. Henri Pirenne, *Medieval Cities: Their Origins and the Revival of Trade*,

trans. Frank D. Halsey (Princeton: Princeton University Press, 1925), p. 218. For the full text of the remarkable 1188 charter at Aire—which begins, "All those who belong in friendship to the town . . ."—see Petr Kropotkin, *Mutual Aid: A Factor of Evolution* (New York: McClure Phillips, 1903), p. 177.

7. Statute of the *Spade compagnia*, cited in Robert D. Putnam with Robert Leonardi and Raffaella Y. Nanetti, *Making Democracy Work: Civic Traditions in Modern Italy* (Princeton: Princeton University Press, 1993), p. 126.

8. Berman, *Law and Revolution*, p. 396.

9. Jean-Paul Sartre, "The Psychology of Imagining," in *Psychology of Imagination* (Citadel Press, 1991), pp. 177–178.

10. For two overviews of the philosophic literature on "the other," see Michael Theunissen, *The Other: Studies in the Social Ontology of Husserl, Heidegger, Sartre, and Buber*, trans. Christopher Macann (Cambridge, Mass.: MIT Press, 1984); and Arleen B. Dallery and Charles E. Scott, eds., *The Question of the Other: Essays in Contemporary Continental Philosophy* (Albany, N.Y.: State University of New York Press, 1989).

11. For a fuller account of this distinction, see Elaine Scarry, "On Vivacity: The Difference between Daydreaming and Imagining-Under-Authorial-Instruction," *Representations* 52 (1995): 72–97.

12. Aleksandr Pushkin, *Eugene Onegin*, rev. ed., trans. Vladimir Nabokov, Bollingen Series LXXII (Princeton: Princeton University Press, 1979), p. 44.

13. W. H. Auden, "In Memory of W. B. Yeats," *Collected Poetry* (New York: Random House, 1945), p. 48.

14. Bertrand Russell, *Unpopular Essays* (New York: Simon and Schuster, 1950), p. 31.

15. John Rawls, *A Theory of Justice* (Cambridge, Mass.: Harvard University Press, 1971), pp. 12, 137.

16. Article I, section 8, clause 11 and the Second Amendment. For a fuller discussion of these two provisions, see Elaine Scarry, "War and the Social Contract: Nuclear Policy, Distribution, and the Right to Bear Arms," *University of Pennsylvania Law Review* 139 (1991): 1257–1316; and "The Declaration of War: Constitutional and Unconstitutional Violence," in *Law's Violence*, eds. A. Sarat and T. Kearns (Ann Arbor: University of Michigan Press, 1992), pp. 23–76. At the time of the writing of the Constitution, the explanations given for these two provisions focused on safeguarding the United States rather than on making foreign populations imaginable. But the two are close: It is by enabling a country to think about the foreign population with whom it may wage war that the home country itself is made safe.

Amartya Sen, Humanity and Citizenship

1. Adam Smith, *The Theory of Moral Sentiments*, eds. D. D. Raphael and A. L. Macfie (1790; reprint, Oxford: Clarendon Press, 1975), p. 140.

2. Smith, *Theory of Moral Sentiments*, pp. 136–137.

3. I have, however, discussed that issue in "Evaluator Relativity and Consequential Evaluation," *Philosophy and Public Affairs* (1993), and in "Well-being, Agency and Freedom: The Dewey Lectures 1984," *Journal of Philosophy* 82 (April 1985).

Martha C. Nussbaum, Reply

1. See J.-J. Rousseau, *Emile*, bk. 4.

2. John Rawls, *A Theory of Justice* (Cambridge, Mass.: Harvard University Press, 1971), p. 3.

3. See my discussion of some of these issues in "Kant and Stoic Cosmopolitanism," in *Journal of Political Philosophy* (forthcoming 1996). On Grotius, see Christopher Ford, "Preaching Propriety to Princes: Grotius, Lipsius, and Neo-Stoic International Law," in *Case Western Reserve Law Journal of International Law* (forthcoming Spring 1996).

4. Himmelfarb (or rather, her history professor) seems wrong in asserting that "the Enlightenment itself had given birth to an aggressive nationalism." The fact that some people living at the time of the Enlightenment were aggressive nationalists hardly makes it right to blame their conduct on thinkers who energetically denounced such projects.

5. *Theory of Justice*, p. 587.

6. Patrick E. Tyler, "U.S. Rights Group Asserts China Lets Thousands of Orphans Die," *New York Times*, 6 January 1996, pp. 1, 4.

7. See *Human Development Report* 1995 (New York: United Nations Development Program, 1995), p. 155. For those interested in the local, the figure for the United States is 76.0, lower than all other countries in the top fifteen in the general ranking, with the exception of Finland, at 75.7, and Germany, at 76.0.

8. On the tradition of religious toleration in India, see Amartya Sen, "Is Coercion a Part of Asian Values?" (forthcoming). Sen establishes that the Indian tradition of toleration is as old as the comparable "Western tradition."

9. Marcus Aurelius did say that Stoicism required one not to be a partisan of the Green or Blue teams at the games—but he was speaking of a Roman context in which such rivalries gave rise to delight in the murder of human beings.

10. See my *Poetic Justice: The Literary Imagination and Public Life* (Boston, Mass.: Beacon Press, 1996).

11. Scott, "The Lay of the Last Minstrel."

12. I am surprised that none of my critics have asked why I focus on the moral claim of the human species, and they appear to neglect the claims of other forms of life. From this direction one could imagine a serious challenge to my position, one that I have not yet answered.

Contributors

Kwame Anthony Appiah is professor of Afro-American Studies and philosophy at Harvard University and author of *In My Father's House: Africa in the Philosophy of Culture* and *Color Conscious* (with Amy Gutmann) (Princeton 1996).

Benjamin R. Barber is Walt Whitman Professor and Director of the Whitman Center for the Culture and Politics of Democracy at Rutgers University, and author most recently of *An Aristocracy of Everyone* (Oxford) and *Jihad vs. McWorld* (Times Books).

Sissela Bok is a Distinguished Fellow at Harvard's Center for Population and Development Studies, and author of several books including *Common Values* (University of Missouri Press).

Judith Butler is professor of rhetoric and comparative literature at the University of California, Berkeley, and is currently writing a book on injurious language.

Joshua Cohen is professor of philosophy and Arthur and Ruth Sloan Professor of Political Science at the Massachusetts Institute of Technology, and editor of *Boston Review*.

Richard Falk is professor of political science at Princeton University.

Nathan Glazer is professor emeritus of education and sociology at Harvard University, the author and editor of books on ethnicity and social policy, and coeditor of *The Public Interest*.

Amy Gutmann is Laurance S. Rockefeller University Professor of Politics and Dean of the Faculty at Princeton University, and author of *Democratic Education, Color Conscious* (with Anthony Appiah), and *Democracy and Disagreement* (with Dennis Thompson).

Gertrude Himmelfarb is professor emeritus at the Graduate School of the City University of New York. Her most recent book is *The De-Moralization of Society: From Victorian Virtues to Modern Values*.

Michael W. McConnell is William B. Graham Professor at the University of Chicago School of Law.

Martha C. Nussbaum is professor of law and ethics at the University of Chicago, and author of several books including *Love's Knowledge, The Fragility of Goodness*, and *Poetic Justice*.

Robert Pinsky teaches at Boston University. His books of poetry include *An Explanation of America* and *The Inferno of Dante*, a verse translation. His most recent book is *The Figured Wheel, New and Collected Poems 1966–1996*.

Hilary Putnam is John Cogan University Professor of Philosophy at Harvard University. His most recent book is *Words and Life*.

Elaine Scarry is professor of English at Harvard University and author of *The Body in Pain* and *Resisting Representation*.

Amartya Sen is professor of economics and philosophy, and Lamont University Professor, at Harvard University. His most recent book is *Inequality Reexamined*.

Charles Taylor is professor of political science and philosophy at McGill University and author of *Sources of the Self* and *Multiculturalism*.

Immanuel Wallerstein is director of the Fernand Braudel Center at the State University of New York, Binghamton, and coauthor of *Race, Nation, Class: Ambiguous Identities.*

Michael Walzer is professor at the Institute for Advanced Study in Princeton and author most recently of *Thick and Thin: Moral Arguments at Home and Abroad.*